Foreword by Archbishop Lawrence Saldanha of Lahore, Pakistan

OUR LORD JESUS repeatedly referred to the violent persecutions that his followers would have to undergo because of his name: "For my sake, you will be brought to trial before rulers and kings to tell the Good News..." (Mt 10:18). From the earliest years, Christians have had to suffer and witness to Jesus even to the supreme sacrifice of their lives. They were called 'martyrs' (witnesses) of Christ, suffering being a living witness of their discipleship. Their names were collected in a book called the 'martyrology', a long and glorious list of the ancient martyrs of the faith.

In our own time there have been countless martyrs of the faith. In particular, the act of witnessing to Christ is to be found among the many minorities living in Islamic lands. There are hundreds of such witnesses – poor and simple souls who have had to endure small and great indignities and humiliations just for living as Christians in a Muslim environment.

My own experience has been that in the first years of the new millennium there is a growing tide of religious intolerance and hatred. It is manifested not just in brutal and violent incidents that catch the headlines but also in subtle and quiet ways that are never reported.

There is a growing need of people living in the West to be more aware of stories of suffering fellow Christians, the more so because this is the price, the 'collateral damage', which they pay vicariously for the greed and iniquities of the Western nations.

I appreciate the support of the charity *Aid to the Church in Need*, which began by helping persecuted people in Eastern Europe and which now helps the suffering minorities in Islamic lands by prayer and by material assistance. Thanks to ACN, they are not alone in their struggles.

This book can form part of a new 'modern martyrology'. These stories must be recorded for posterity so that they may inspire future generations and give them courage to be strong and heroic witnesses of Christ's love and compassion in difficult circumstances.

\+ Lawrence J. Saldanha, Archbishop of Lahore, Pakistan

3

Contents

Introduction 5
Afghanistan 9
Bangladesh 11
Belarus 13
Bosnia–Herzegovina 15
Burma 17
China 19
Interview with Cardinal Joseph Zen of Hong Kong 24
Cuba 27
Cuba – A break-through on the airwaves 28
Egypt 30
India 32
Indonesia (and East Timor) 35
Iran 38
Iraq 40
Interview with Archbishop Louis Sako of Kirkuk 44
Israel/Palestine 47
Laos 52
Nigeria 54
North Korea 58
Pakistan 61
Interview with Yusif Said, a Christian from Pakistan ...66
Russia 68
Saudi Arabia 71
Sri Lanka 73
Sudan 77
Interview with Bishop Daniel Adwok of Khartoum 81
Turkey 84
Vietnam 87
Zimbabwe 90
Introducing *Aid to the Church in Need* 95

Introduction

"IT IS A MIRACLE that our church survived – this has only been possible by God's grace. The past week has been a time of destruction and great fear. We all know there was a violent demonstration on the road outside and thousands of people were causing harm and destruction."

Such were the words of the Most Rev Lawrence Saldanha, Archbishop of Lahore, east Pakistan. Sat in the congregation, it was difficult to believe what we were hearing. Nor did it seem possible that it was being said by an archbishop in his own cathedral. Of neo-Romanesque style, the fine structure in which we were sitting seemed invincible, a monument to peace and tranquillity. And yet this was not Western Europe, it was Pakistan and just a few days earlier, an estimated 100,000 people had crammed into the streets of the city of Lahore shouting obscenities against the West and against Christians. Armed with explosives and other weapons, they were intent on causing maximum disruption.

Eventually, the police arrived and dispersed the crowds using tear gas. And yet, as Archbishop Saldanha explained, although the immediate crisis had passed, a palpable sense of fear and confusion remained.

To our amazement, Archbishop Saldanha then held up a book chronicling acts of oppression against Christians. The book, called *Violence against Christians* was produced by Dr J G Orbán de Lengyelfalva of *Aid to the Church in Need*, the charity for the persecuted and oppressed Church. The archbishop said: "Fortunately, we have people who are concerned about us, people who are in solidarity with us and who are praying with us." Few gestures could have done more to underline the importance of standing shoulder to shoulder with those who are despised for their religious beliefs and whose whole way of life is under threat.

Building on the success of *Violence against Christians*, ACN's *Persecuted and Forgotten? A Report on Christians oppressed for their Faith 2005/2006* is a tribute to the courageous many who suffer for what they believe. Be it in Pakistan, North Korea, China or Sudan, the people's great fear is that their suffering is being ignored by the West – by the very people who can make a difference and who in many cases brought Christianity to them in the first place. By telling their story, many are risking their lives. For them, that risk is the defining mark of authenticity. In 2005 after 25

5

years of leading his people in a country with Islamic *Shari'a* law, Sudan's Cardinal Gabriel Zubeir Wako told ACN supporters in London: "If I say that Christians are persecuted, how long is it going to take to get people to trust me? How many people realise that in speaking I am putting my life at stake?" The cardinal was echoing statements made on several occasions by the Sudanese bishops in meetings with international groups.

So, what do we mean by the term 'persecution'? In which countries are Christians persecuted and why? Overuse has emptied the word 'persecution' of its original meaning. In keeping with the *Oxford Dictionary* definition, persecution, so far as this study is concerned, is taken to mean a malicious act motivated by religious hostility.

This sets the criteria for the material included in this book. The mere fact that a priest has been killed does not necessarily qualify for entry. What changes things is if reports indicate that religion was a motivating factor. In some cases, religion may be one of many such factors but that does not disqualify such incidents from inclusion, it simply sets them in a particular context.

International events have, sadly, seen religious fundamentalism become a leading force for ill in the world. And in reflecting the down-turn in world stability, this book identifies three key factors which explain why persecution against Christians is an increasing menace threatening the long-term survival of the Church in key parts of the world.

- Militant Islam:

The threat now posed by fundamentalist Muslims has specific and terrible implications for Christian communities especially in Islamic countries. Islamic *Shari'a* law's thorough-going oppression of non-Muslims is largely unknown to the West. Harsh sentences, including death, are meted out for apostasy (converting to a faith outside Islam) and for insults against the Prophet Mohammed. Life imprisonment can follow charges of defacing the *Qur'an*.

In an environment where Christianity is strongly refuted, Christians are often first in line for allegations of this kind. Anti-Christian propaganda is sometimes preached in mosques, occasionally with violent consequences for Christians. *Shari'a* enforces a costly property tax for non-Muslims.

Building of churches and outdoor non-Muslim worship is sometimes prohibited, as is the public display of crosses. Women, who are severely discriminated against regardless of their religion, fare far worse if they are Christians. The law offers virtually no protection for Christian women and as a result rape and other forms of physical abuse are widespread.

Countries affected: Afghanistan, Bangladesh, Egypt, Indonesia (and East Timor), Iran, Iraq, Israel (Palestine), (Northern) Nigeria, Pakistan, Saudi Arabia, (Northern) Sudan, Turkey.

- Radical Hinduism and Buddhism:

Contrary to popular belief whereby Buddhists and Hindus are seen as universally peaceful, some countries suffer at the hands of extremists from both religions. Nationalist and religious agendas have merged in a bid to stifle the growth of so-called alien influences such as Christianity, which is seen as an unwanted legacy of the colonial era. Largely unreported in the main media are the attacks on Christians and how they are threatened by new anti-conversion laws. Human rights organisations are increasingly concerned about the impact of the laws, especially as in some cases they are geared specifically towards discriminating against Christians.

Countries affected: India, Sri Lanka.

- Dictatorial regimes:

Communist countries which survived the break-up of the USSR in the late 1980s and early 1990s have faced a tough choice: change or die. For many, this has meant, at least at some level, rehabilitating religious groups by scrapping a hard-line atheistic philosophy. But in reality the old practices remain – spying, house arrests, imprisonment, mysterious disappearances, violence and even executions. Totalitarian-style controls continue to affect the daily life of the Church, limiting or banning freedom of speech (access to the media) and interference in the appointment of bishops.

Countries affected: Belarus, Burma, Cuba, China, Laos, Russia, Vietnam, Zimbabwe.

These three key factors – militant Islam, radical Hinduism and Buddhism, and dictatorial regimes – define the contents of this book. Selected here are 24 countries where Christians suffer for the faith they profess. While the book concentrates on countries where Christians suffer the most, to obtain a more global perspective, *Persecuted and Forgotten?* also assesses a number of countries where, in spite of extensive media coverage, the rights of religious minorities have received little or no air-time. In many instances, the book provides a unique glimpse into the life of Christians in places almost completely cut off from the West. Where the veil of secrecy lifts, it is often because of ACN's unique relationship with bishops all over the world. The book draws extensively from two similar publications, also produced by *Aid to the Church in Need*, which both report on the persecution of Christians – the Italian *Rapporto 2006 sulla Libertà Religiosa nel Mondo*, and the French *Persécutions antichrétiennes dans le monde*. Research has also involved other organisations concerned with religious freedom as well as news agencies. While every effort has been made to vouch for the accuracy of the material contained here, it cannot be guaranteed.

Central to this book's objective is to bear out the claim that Christians are probably the most persecuted religious group in the world. Reports suggest that every year 170,000 Christians are killed for religious reasons. In the last century, it is thought that 45 million Christians died as the victims of religious/cultural hatred, but no reliable figures are available for the start of the new millennium because of the volatile world situation. What is clear is that religious freedom has suddenly and quite dramatically come under threat in many countries where for decades, even centuries, it was taken for granted. In more than 50 countries around the globe, Christians face grave and sometimes life-threatening risks on account of their faith.

For Christians in these countries – and others besides – *Aid to the Church in Need* is a spiritual lifeline. The charity remains true to the spirit of its founder, Father Werenfried van Straaten, who famously said: "Our work consists in drying the tears of God wherever he weeps." Published in the 60th year of ACN's existence, the book reflects the charity's efforts to build on its founder's legacy. More than 43 million copies of ACN's *Child's Bible* have been distributed in 150 languages worldwide; ACN supports thousands of seminarians and novices; churches are being built, refugees are being helped to flee persecution, and the daily needs of poor priests and sisters are being met through Mass stipends and other forms of aid.

In its mission to shine a light for Christians in their darkest hour, ACN responded to more than 5,000 requests for aid in 2005. Through this work of prayer, information and action, the charity ensures that persecuted Christians are not forgotten.

Afghanistan

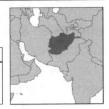

Population	Religions	Christian Population
20 million	*Sunni* Muslim 80% *Shi'a* Muslim 19% Others 1%	Less than 2,500

Before the Taliban were overthrown in 2001, Afghanistan was a hard-line Islamic state and *Shari'a* law was strictly enforced. As President, Hamid Karzai was charged with introducing greater freedoms. Humanitarian aid by non-Muslim NGOs was soon permitted but was closely supervised. In 2003, there were reports that two Christian volunteers were murdered for having 'evangelised' Muslims. Karzai, who headed the provisional administration established when the Taliban were forced from power, won Afghanistan's first direct presidential elections in October 2004. Earlier that same year, a constitution was drawn up which enshrined personal freedoms and which recognised the Universal Declaration of Human Rights, the document guaranteeing the individual the right to choose their own religion. But the constitution also draws from both civil and Islamic *Shari'a* laws and explicitly states that no law can "contravene the tenets and provisions" of Islam. Experts claim the constitution is deliberately ambiguous and sets out to address the concerns of both reformists and the conservatives. The constitution's apparent contradictions leave it open to being exploited by growing extremist factions who are determined to clamp down on supposedly non-Islamic infiltration. The Christian presence in Afghanistan is minimal, all the more so because of the discretion of its adherents. There is only one official place of Christian worship – in the Italian embassy.

June/July 2005: Five Afghans who had converted to Christianity were assassinated. The reports also stated that the attackers also killed a *Mullah* (Muslim theologian and Islamic lawyer) who was considered too tolerant.[1]

October 2005: The head of the Church's mission in Afghanistan, Monsignor Giuseppe Moretti, spoke of the Afghan Government's "willingness" to open relations with the Vatican. Among the "important" signs of hope he listed was Afghan President Hamid Karzai's attendance at the funeral of Pope John Paul II, six months earlier. Monsignor Moretti

9

reported that Kabul government officials had said it would be "an honour" to welcome the Sisters of Charity (Mother Teresa Sisters), who had been hoping to go to Afghanistan.

March 2006: Abdul Rahman, aged 41, who had been charged with apostasy for converting from Islam to Christianity, was given asylum in Italy. There was an international outcry after the media reported that he faced possible execution for his religious beliefs. Mr Rahman was allegedly reported to the authorities after returning to Afghanistan a few years ago to seek custody for his two daughters. Mr Rahman, who became a Christian 16 years earlier while working as an aid worker for an international Christian organisation, was arrested after police discovered him with a Bible. Pope Benedict XVI led a campaign for his release from trial. In a letter to Afghan President Hamid Karzai, the Pope wrote that dropping the case "would bestow great honour upon the Afghan people and would raise a chorus of admiration in the international community". Arriving in Italy after escaping the Afghan courts, Mr Rahman told journalists: "If you are not a Muslim in an Islamic country like mine, they kill you, make no mistake."[2] According to Italian interior ministry officials, Mr Rahman was moved to a safe location elsewhere in the country. Politicians in Afghanistan hit out against Mr Rahman's release saying his escape from trial was "contrary to the laws … in Afghanistan". They condemned the West's "interference" on his behalf.

Bangladesh

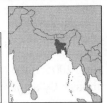

Population	Religions	Christian Population
153 million[3]	Muslims 84% Hindu 14% Buddhists 1% Christians 1%.	1.5 million

Islamic fundamentalism has found fertile ground in a country racked by poverty and crippled by exponential population growth. In the last 25 years, population statistics for the capital, Dhaka, show a rise from 2.2 million to 12 million.[4] Islamist influence has tightened its grip and Bangladesh's first woman Prime Minister, Khaleda Zia, was forced to act, especially after hundreds of bomb attacks in August 2005. A number of 'most-wanted' terrorists have since been arrested. It is a small start. According to the *Far Eastern Economic Review*, there are over 50,000 Islamic extremists in the country belonging to more than 40 terrorist groups trained in 50 camps across Bangladesh. Questions are being asked about the willingness of the authorities to root out extremism. According to Charles Tannock, vice president of the Human Rights Committee of the European Parliament, religious extremists appear to be acting with the "apparent support of the police, the local authorities and of the ruling party" – the Bangladeshi National Party (BNP). Bangladesh was considered a lay and secular state but after the BNP came to power in 2001, there was a dramatic shift towards radicalism. The *Jamaat-e-Islami* Party, a member of the governing coalition, demanded the imposition of *Shari'a* Islamic law and encouraged the building of thousands of *Madrassa* Islamic schools.

March 2005: A Baptist minister was murdered by armed men from an extremist Muslim group, allegedly the *Jamaat-e-Islami*.[5] Three of the killers were arrested but were later released after pressure from a local MP. Reports indicated a lack of progress in tracking down the killers both of the minister and a Christian doctor, Abdul Gani, murdered on 18 September 2004, even though their identity is thought to be known to the police.

July 2005: The backlash on Muslims in Britain following the July 7th bomb attacks in London led to concerns of possible attacks on churches in Bangladesh. Police in the capital, Dhaka, met Christian leaders to discuss options to tighten security.[6] Armed forces placed 24-hour guards at

11

Dhaka's Catholic cathedral. Police asked for a list of Christian buildings thought to be at risk. Church leaders requested that the security measures be implemented nation-wide.

June 2005: Two (Protestant) Christians were murdered in their sleep, apparently as punishment for taking part in Christian activities. They were reportedly threatened by a member of a local *Madrassa* (Islamic school).

August 2005: The Bengali language daily newspaper *Ittefaq* published a report by security forces identifying three non-Muslim buildings as under threat from terrorists. Among them was the Church of the Holy Rosary, which was named alongside the Kamalpur Buddhist monastery in Dhaka and the Hindu Dhakeshwari Temple.

August 2005: Bishop Moses Costa from the northern diocese of Dinajpur said militant Muslims in Bangladesh were using the US-led War on Terror as an excuse to spread fear among Christians.[7] In an ACN interview, in which he described Christians as "frightened" and anxious to flee abroad, he said job discrimination, seizure of Christian property and intimidation were now commonplace. He said: "The [fundamentalist Muslims] take the view that the Christians are to blame for what has happened to Muslims in places like Palestine and Iraq. The US–UK action in the Middle East is seen as fighting against Muslims. That is why the [Islamists] are causing difficulties here for minority groups."

Bishop Costa, whose diocese borders Nepal, said that a few months previously he had been forced to intervene after local Islamic authorities demolished a Christian village only to win European Union funding to replace it with an 'ideal Muslim' one. The EU withdrew the funding after the bishop persuaded one of its officials to fly to Bangladesh to verify his claim that the Muslim village was not being built on virgin land. Bishop Costa said: "65 families were left homeless after that village was completely destroyed. People had been living there for at least 100 years. At least the EU funding has now been stopped."

December 2005: The threat from Islamic militants forced clergy at Holy Rosary parish, Dhaka diocese, to hold Midnight Mass early. Parish priest Fr Gomes warned people against entering the church with rucksacks and to report any strange behaviour. According to news sources, Fr Gomes had received threatening telephone calls warning of bomb explosions during the Christmas celebrations.[8]

Belarus

Population	Religions	Christian Population
10 million	Christians 70.1%[9] Non religious 24% Atheists 4.9% Others 1%	7 million

The regime installed at the end of 1994 by President Alexander Lukashenko continues to exert strict controls over every sphere of life in Belarus. Not for nothing is the country often referred to as one of the 'last dictatorships' in the former Soviet empire. The USA and EU condemned as flawed the March 2006 elections in which Lukashenko emerged victorious, claiming 80 percent of the vote.

Religious freedom is enshrined in the constitution, but this is not the case in reality. After the fall of the USSR, the regime that emerged in Belarus soon began treating the major Churches very differently. The effect of the 2002 Religion Laws was to split them up into three categories. Highly favoured and supported was the Russian Orthodox Church, registered and tolerated were the Catholic Church and the traditional Protestant communities. But effectively outlawed were the relatively new evangelical groups which were keen to seize the advantage after the fall of communism. Even worship in private is a punishable offence for the new Churches. For the Catholic communities, issues of religious freedom are still overshadowed by the close relationship between the Orthodox and the State. It was widely reported that before giving permission to requests from the Catholic Church, President Lukashenko was known to consult the Orthodox head – Metropolitan Filaret, the patriarchal exarch of Belarus. For the time being, however, the Catholic Church is able to consolidate its position thanks to the good relationship its bishops have developed with their Orthodox counterparts. This relationship is key to the future of the Catholic Church in Belarus.

March 2005: In an interview, Jurij Gorulev, president of the Catholic Association for Communications in Belarus, praised President Lukashenko for taking positive steps towards the Latin-rite Catholic Church.[10] He described how the President had joined in the celebrations marking the 90th birthday of Belarus primate Cardinal Kazimierz Swiatek in October 2004.

Mr Gorulev said problems for the Catholic media in Belarus were confined to recruiting technical staff and persuading the country's media to take an interest in the Church.

Spring 2005: Just four months after their previous meeting, Cardinal Swiatek met President Lukashenko a second time to ask for the return of Catholic churches confiscated during the Soviet era and permission to build new churches, especially in the outskirts of large cities. Cardinal Swiatek publicly handed him a letter from Pope John Paul II, the contents of which were not made public, and discussed with him a series of problems concerning the current situation in Belarus. Among other things these included "the restitution of the churches confiscated by the Soviet regime and the construction of new buildings for religious worship, above all on the outskirts of the large cities, where many people are flooding in". The greatest problem is the construction of churches in Minsk.

December 2005: A presidential decree provided a tax exemption for religious organisations registered with the government.[11] The ruling proposed a tax exemption on properties used for religious purposes. Further tax breaks were set in place for liturgical literature and furnishings specifically intended for religious worship. A statement from the President's press office said that the tax exemptions were intended to free up Church finances for social, educational and humanitarian activities.

April 2005: The European Religious Liberty Forum, made up of lawyers, journalists and human rights activists from across Europe have complained about the imprisonment of two Christian leaders in Belarus.[12] Pastor Georgi Vladimirovich Vyazovsky and human rights lawyer Sergey Shavtsov received a 10-day prison sentence. Pastor Vyazovsky was charged with holding regular religious meetings in his private home without permission from the local authorities. Sergey Shavtsov, a human rights lawyer, was arrested on 24 March 2006 and jailed for organising a religious event, an inter-denominational conference, without government permission. On the last day of the conference, three policemen and one KGB officer burst in and alleged that the event was against the law. They cited the 2002 legislation On Freedom of Conscience and the Religious Organisations.

Bosnia–Herzegovina

Population	Religions	Christian Population
4.2 million	Muslims 45% Christians 47% Others 8%	2 million

The inter-ethnic war of the 1990s left Bosnia–Herzegovina in tatters and more than a decade after the conflict ended, the country is still recovering. Within just three years, 250,000 people died in the clashes between Bosnian Muslims, Croats and Serbs. After an uneasy truce, the Dayton Accord of 1995 firstly recognised within the one country of Bosnia–Herzegovina a republic formed of Orthodox Serbs and secondly approved a federation made up of Muslims and Croats.[13]

With a new settlement in place enforced by peace keepers from across Europe, the accord set out to enable the many people displaced during the war to return to their homelands. But the Catholics, who represent 14 percent of the population, have grown increasingly critical of the international community for neglecting them and concentrating their aid mainly on the Muslims. The Catholics claim they are treated unfairly and according to reports 60 percent of young people wish to emigrate to the West because they see no future in Bosnia.

Before the war, Muslims in Bosnia were comparatively peaceful and secular but soon after the conflict broke out many fundamentalists entered the country. *Wahibi* Islamists are seeking to widen their influence in Bosnian society. Considerable amounts of aid have come from Arabic countries, but only for Muslims. For example in Mostar, the main city of Herzegovina, 40 mosques were built after the war. This has intimidated the Christian community who have left for other countries.

The country is suffering from profound social problems, including unemployment at close on 40 percent, illiteracy at around 15 percent and one person in five is surviving on about US$1 a day. The problems are compounded by high crime levels and random acts of intolerance towards minority religious groups. Reports have come in of people – including many priests – receiving insults and living in fear of attacks.

February 2005: Church leaders reported that the number of Catholics in Bosnia–Herzegovina had fallen by half in less than a generation.[14] According to the statistics, there were one million Catholics before conflict engulfed Bosnia in the 1990s. Within 15 years, numbers have fallen to barely 500,000. Releasing the figures, Fr Mijo Dzolan said the emigration had come in response to widespread unrest and religious discrimination since the 1995 Dayton Accord. Controversially, the accord accepted the presence of a Serb Republic but added a Muslim–Croat federation in Bosnia, decreeing that the country as a whole would remain a single state.

November 2005: Bishop Franjo Komarica of Banja Luka, in the north of the country, accused international organisations such as the European Union and the UN of systematic discrimination against Bosnia's Catholics.[15] The bishop claimed that the Catholics were being systematically prevented from returning to their homes in the wake of the war. In an interview, Bishop Komarica said: "By its behaviour, the international community is still blocking the return of Catholic Croats to Bosnia. So far, international institutions are rewarding the unjust and punishing the disadvantaged." Of the 220,000 Catholics who lived in the Republika Srpska territory of Bosnia–Herzegovina before the Balkans war, only about 12,000 remained, said the bishop.[16] He called on the international community to "act with more unity, more honesty, more credibility and more justice when implementing international law". The bishop's statement echoes another made in October 2005 by the President of the Catholic bishops' conference of Bosnia–Herzegovina, Cardinal Vinko Puljic.

Summer 2006: Investigations uncovered serious problems building a place of worship in Bosnia–Herzegovina.[17] Religious communities of all faiths face obstruction in getting permission to build or re-build places of worship. For example, in the Bosnian-controlled area, mosques have been built without official permission. The reports indicated that Catholic and Protestant churches face years of official obstruction. In the Croat-controlled area, especially in and around Mostar, Muslim and Protestant places of worship cannot be built legally. In the Serb-controlled area, Serbian Orthodox churches can be built, but places of worship of other faiths can face much obstruction.

Burma

Population	Religions	Christian Population
51 million	Buddhists 72.6%, Animists 12.6%, Christians 8.3%, Muslims 2.4%, Others 4.1%	4.2 million

Burma – also known as Myanmar – is ruled by a military junta that ruthlessly stamps out any hint of opposition to its rule. Largely impenetrable to outsiders, Burma's government assumes a position of absolute power, defying international pressure and severe sanctions. Aung San Suu Kyi from the National League for Democracy was the outright winner of the 1990 parliamentary elections – the last to be held in the country – but the military junta refused to hand over power after nullifying the results.

The country's devastating human rights record is strictly off limits for the media, which is heavily censored and puts out a strictly on-message news agenda consistent with government policy.

In the 1960s, almost all foreign missionaries were expelled from the country. All the schools and hospitals under their control were swiftly nationalised. The country is covered with symbols of a rich Buddhist heritage but even followers of this, Burma's majority religion, suffer at the hands of the regime. For religious minorities, the situation is far worse, and Christians and Muslims bear the brunt of systematic and indiscriminate attacks.

There is considerable suspicion of Christians because many of them belong to the ethnic groups responsible for the most serious insurrections against government rule. According to some reports, Christians make up 40 percent of the Karen people who are among those most vocal in demanding democracy.[18] There are also many Christians among the Kachin in the north of Burma and among the Chin and the Naga in the west. According to the association Christian Freedom International, which helps the persecuted ethnic minorities by collecting and providing food and medicines, this repression reaches a peak in the month of April. It coincides with the dry season when the soldiers are able to move around more easily in the dense Burmese jungle.[19]

The government imposes restrictions on the Church's evangelisation work, on the construction of churches, and on the import and distribution of Christian books. In addition, the ruling military junta monitors religious activities in a bid to nip democracy movements in the bud.

April 2005: A nun, whose identity has to be protected for her own safety, said Burma's military government was preventing the Church from carrying out its mission.[20] She said the ordinary faithful sometimes had difficulty getting the prayer books and catechisms. She said many Catholics of Burma knew little or nothing about the reforms of the Second Vatican Council, even 40 years after it happened, because when it concluded in 1965, the military dictatorship had already been in power for three years. "It is extremely expensive to print books and we do not have advanced technologies. Again, it is extremely difficult to obtain material for the simple reason that it does not exist. The texts we do have are old and out of date; we need new ones. We also need to find a way of staying in contact with the Universal Church. A spiritual guide is a primary necessity and is much longed for, especially by young people."

June 2006: The Burma Army continued its offensive in Karen State, the biggest military assault since 1997.[21] Eyewitnesses reported further killings, burning of villages, the capture of civilians, including children, and the use of forced labour. According to the latest reports from the Free Burma Rangers, a relief team working in the east of the country, the number of displaced people in Karen State rose to over 18,000. In one area, over 800 civilians have been captured and forced to work as porters for the military, along with over 1,000 prisoners. In the latest reported attack, the Burma Army's Light Infantry Battalion 362 attacked and burned Ger Baw Kee village in north-western Muthraw District on 2 June. The previous day, Naw Yo Hta and Kay Pu villages suffered a third day of mortar attacks, by three Burma Army battalions.

China

Population	Religions	Christian Population
1.3 billion	Atheist 50%, Chinese religions 29%, Buddhists 8%, Christians 6%, Others 7%	80 million[22]

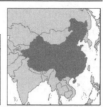

After years of controversy and criticism about human rights and religious freedom in China, the communist authorities have set about a new initiative to change world opinion. It is this that lies behind the New Regulations on Religious Activities, released in March 2005.[23] The new regulations re-draw the dividing line between religious activities judged permissible and those banned by the State.

However, none of this has prevented the government from continuing its policy of Church oppression – arresting Christian faithful and their religious leaders, torturing people, destroying and confiscating places of worship, banning the education of the young, prohibiting bishops and priests from travelling and preventing Chinese citizens from contact with the outside world.

Part of the reason for the continued oppression of the Church is the ambiguity of the New Regulations. The document stresses that 'normal' religious activities are permitted but only later does it become clear that 'normal' in this instance means those under State control. Everything else is defined as 'delinquent'. So it is that while asserting the Church's rights on the one hand, the Chinese authorities take them away with the other.

Perhaps one reason for the authorities' ambivalence is that within the Communist Party, about 20 million members, one third of the total, follow some form of religious faith, even though officially they are meant to be atheist. According to China's President Hu Jintao, the situation is "undermining communists' belief in the party" and "plunging the ... State into further political and social chaos."[24]

Existing in a context in which government political activism is mixed with philosophical ambivalence, the Church in China often appears to take a step forward only to find itself going one back.

One reason for this is that religious liberty exists in theory but because all Church communities have to be registered, they are controlled by the

Communist Party. Bibles are not officially banned in China, but they have to be printed by Chinese printing presses. Foreign missionaries have no freedom of movement. There are numerous arrests but it is impossible to guess how many.

The Catholic Church in China is made up of two parts. Up to two thirds of China's 15 million[25] Catholics belong to the 'Underground' Church. Its bishops are appointed by Rome but they are not recognised by the State. The 'Official' Church by contrast is recognised by Beijing and its bishops are approved by the government. The Holy See now recognises more than three-quarters of the 'Official' Church's 74 bishops. Discussions have taken place between Beijing and Rome and among the issues raised was the status of the 'Underground' Church. Beijing is demanding the end of diplomatic relations between the Vatican and Taiwan and the 'non-interference in China's internal religious affairs'. At the time of going to press, at least two bishops were in prison – Bishop Giacomo su Zhimin of Baoding and his Auxiliary, Bishop Francesco An Shuxin – while at least 13 others were prevented from exercising their ministry. Around 20 priests were either imprisoned or reported missing. They stand accused of celebrating Mass/preaching a retreat.

Christmas 2004: In Linjiayuan, a village in the Zhejiang province, the police intervened to stop preparations for Christmas Midnight Mass. Fr Jean Wang, a priest of the 'Underground' Church, was arrested. But as soon as the police left, the Catholic faithful, who numbered about 2,000, returned to the church and went ahead with the celebrations as best they could in the absence of their priest. Latest reports showed that after several months in prison, Fr Jean still had not been released.

January 2005: 'Underground' Bishop Julius Jia Zhiguo of Zhengding was arrested and released shortly after. The bishop, whose diocese is in Hebei province, south of Beijing, has already spent 20 years in prison for his refusal to join the 'Official' Church. The bishop was arrested again in July 2005 and was held for a few days. He was forced to undergo 'study' – brain-washing sessions to force him to join the Patriotic Association. In November 2005 there were more reports of his arrest by Chinese government security officials.[26] According to sources in China, the officials asked him to bring clothes and then drove him to Shijiazhuang city. ACN

UK National Director Neville Kyrke-Smith, who met Bishop Zhiguo in China, commented on how the arrest had coincided with the visit to London of China's President Hu Jintao. "At the very moment when President Hu meets [British Prime Minister] Tony Blair in London and the town is painted red, it is ironic that the dark side of the neo-communist regime is revealed in all its sinister colours." Reports claimed that Bishop Zhiguo was arrested eight times since January 2004.

March 2005: New laws were introduced which limit the penalties for breach of China's strict rulings on religious activities. The rules allow for people to petition for the release of imprisoned clergy. Observers say the rulings will be routinely ignored by over-zealous law enforcers.

March 2005: Agencies such as *Asia News* and the Holy Spirit Study Centre, Hong Kong, called for the release of 19 bishops and 18 priests held in detention centres, labour camps or under house arrest. The agencies published a list of clergy whom they believed were being detained.

March 2005: Fr Zhao Kexun was arrested while celebrating Mass at home. Reports said he was a close collaborator of 'Underground' Bishop Zhao Zhendong of Xuanjua, of whom nothing was heard since his arrest in December 2004. The next day, 80-year-old Bishop Yao Liang of Xiwanzi diocese, in the Hebei province, was also arrested. He was ordered to deny Rome but he refused to do so.

May 2005: Catholics marked the anniversary of the disappearance of Bishop Shi Enxiang, who went missing aged 79 exactly four years previously. Beijing has denied all knowledge of his whereabouts. Catholics have expressed fears that Bishop Enxiang died in prison.

May 2005: Beijing reiterated its commitment to opening diplomatic relations with the Vatican but once again spelled out that the offer was conditional on the Holy See ceasing to recognise Taiwan.

June 2005: Fr Zhao Kexun, 75, was freed after two months in prison.

July 2005: A Protestant pastor was arrested for possession of Bibles that had not been printed in China.

October 2005: Four bishops from China were prevented from flying to Rome to take part in a Synod, which Pope Benedict XVI had invited them to attend.[27] At the request of the Vatican, four chairs stood empty for the duration of the Synod on the Eucharist, held from 2–23 October. Invitations to the synod were sent to Archbishop Anthony Li Duan of Xian, and Bishop Aloysius Jin Luxian of Shanghai, both of whom are recognised by the government. Another invitation was issued to Bishop Luke Li Jingfeng of Fengxiang (Shaanxi), who was recognised by the government in 2004. Also invited was Bishop Joseph Wei Jingyi of Qiqihar, not recognised by the government.[28] At a Mass at St Peter's in Rome, at the end of the synod, the Pope expressed regret that the four bishops were not present and said the church in China was still on a "suffering path".[29] Beijing gave no official justification for refusing to allow the bishops to attend the synod.

October 2005: Bishop Peter Zhang Bairen of Hanyang died aged 91. The bishop was very loyal to the Pope and spent 24 years in confinement – either in prison or forced labour camps. Initially, the government said both 'Underground' and 'Official' clergy were allowed at his funeral. The day before the service, on 15 October, the police ordered the faithful not to attend and to honour the bishop only as "Mr Shang".[30] At least 7,000 people defied the order and attended the Mass. Thousands of others were stopped outside the city, their path blocked by the police.

November 2005: On an official visit to China, US President George W. Bush visited Gangwashi church, a state-recognised Protestant church and spoke up for persecuted Christians. Addressing the press after the service, he said: "My hope is that the government of China will not fear Christians who gather to worship openly."

November 2005: Six 'Underground' priests from Zhen Ding diocese were arrested – Fathers Guo Zhijun, aged 36, Zhang Xiuchi, 60, Peng Jianjun, 30, Zhang Yinhu, 45, Wang Jin Shan and Gao Lingshen, 50. Some of the priests were also beaten.

November 2005: Forty thugs severely beat 16 sisters of the Franciscan Missionaries of the Sacred Heart in Xian, in Shaanxi province. All of the sisters were taken to hospital. One of them lost her sight in one eye and another had a delicate operation on her spine. The sisters were trying to prevent the demolition of a school that belonged to the congregation and which the town authorities had sold to a development company.

November 2005: Fr Gao Baojin, the rector of the seminary in the diocese of Zhaoxian in Hebei, was arrested by staff from the Religious Affairs Office and was forced to undergo indoctrination on the religious policy of the party. He was targeted after giving hospitality to 'Underground' church seminarians. Seven deacons at his seminary were also arrested and were forced to attend indoctrination courses before their release on 3 December. They were forbidden to sleep, go to the toilet or take medication. The officials who kidnapped them tried to force them to sign a form accepting to be ordained as priests by a government-appointed bishop rather than one in communion with Rome. The seminarians did not yield.

December 2005: About 30 men beat up around 50 Christians – both priests and lay people – in Tianjin. The Catholics had come from neighbouring dioceses to defend the Church's rights regarding a building in the area.

December 2005: 'Underground' Bishop Han Dingxian of Yongnian, Hebei, was reported missing. After 1999, he had been held in isolation at a government hotel and denied contacts with friends and family.

February 2006: Bishop Joseph Zen-kiun of Hong Kong, a sometimes fierce critic of the Chinese government, was created a cardinal, prompting reports of disquiet from the Communist authorities. **(See Interview with Cardinal Joseph Zen of Hong Kong, page 24)**.

April and May 2006: The Vatican protested after the 'Official' Church went ahead with two episcopal ordinations despite having no approval from Rome. The Chinese Patriotic Association (CPA) on 30 April ordained Fr Ma Yinglin as Bishop of Kunming, in China's south-western Yunnan province. Barely three days later, in Anhui province, central China, Fr Liu Xinhong was ordained bishop. On 7 May, an episcopal ordination went ahead, apparently this time with Vatican approval. Fr Paul Pei Junmin was ordained Auxiliary Bishop of Shenyang, the biggest city in north-east China. Hong Kong's Cardinal Zen criticised the "illicit" ordinations and called for a halt to dialogue between China and the Vatican. He described the appointments as "a slap in the face against the Vatican".[31] Cardinal Zen told the BBC that Beijing had imposed a "fait accompli". He continued: "By appointing their own bishops hastily and illegally, [the CPA] have tried to impose their own selection on the Vatican. This shows disregard for the spirit of negotiation and disrupts mutual trust."[32] Beijing said the Vatican had no right to interfere in China's internal affairs.

Interview with Cardinal Joseph Zen of Hong Kong

Zenit, Milan, Italy
5 June 2006

BISHOP JOSEPH ZEN-KIUN'S bold and unrelenting efforts to speak up for the suffering Church in China received official recognition when Pope Benedict XVI created him a cardinal at the Pontiff's first consistory on 24 March 2006.

A sometimes fierce critic of the government, the Bishop of Hong Kong has taken full advantage of the former British colony's until now semi-independent relationship with the Chinese mainland, which has enabled him to speak out far more than his brother bishops.

Receiving his 'red hat' at the ceremony of cardinals in Rome was a far cry from his beginnings in life. Born in Shanghai in 1931 and ordained priest aged about 30, he was a professor at several seminaries of the 'Official' and 'Underground' Church across China. He was named Coadjutor Bishop of Hong Kong in 1996 and bishop of the same diocese in 2002. He has care of 250,000 Catholics from a total population in Hong Kong of seven million.

Soon after becoming a cardinal, he gave an interview which was carried by *Zenit* Catholic (Vatican) news agency. Referring to his new robes as cardinal, he explained: "The colour red that I wear means the willingness of a cardinal to shed his own blood. But it is not my blood which has been shed; it is the blood and tears of numerous nameless heroes of the 'Official' and 'Underground' Church, who suffered for being faithful to the Church."

Q: How many nameless heroes are there of the Church in China?

Cardinal Zen: Some have tried to make this calculation but it seems impossible to me to give an exact number. The only certain thing is that there have been very many. Many died in prison, in concentration camps and in forced labour. Many others died of serious sicknesses contracted in prison.

There are also those who have survived 20–30 years in prison and tortures; they too are martyrs. It is a form of modern martyrdom. It is not crucifixion or immediate violent death but a very long suffering, endured in many years of isolation.

There are people who entered a prison or concentration camp when they were younger than 20 and left when they were elderly and with ruined health. I am thinking of many youths of the Legion of Mary, who went to prison in Shanghai in the '50s, the majority laymen rather than priests or nuns, who do not have a family to think about. And yet, I have seen many of them leave the prisons with joy and serenity – a great testimony.

But we must not forget the sufferings of the families either. Imagine parents who see a child snatched from them, without ever again knowing where he is or what befell him.

Q: One often hears that the situation has improved today.

Cardinal Zen: It depends what is meant. No doubt, the Chinese regime, which has more exchanges with the outside [world] today … must be more careful, less brutal. For example, bishops who are arrested don't go to prison but to isolated places; their detention is not as long. This does not deny the fact that the two bishops of Baoding [city] have disappeared and their whereabouts are unknown.

I would say, however, that the most important evolution is happening within the 'Official' Church itself, with an ever clearer communion with the Pope. And one sees that, when the priests are united, even the regime must give way, as demonstrated by the appointments for Shanghai and Xian [dioceses]: proposed by the Pope but formally chosen by the local clergy – the government was not able to say anything.

Q: Also in your Diocese of Hong Kong, you are often in the limelight because of your firm position in defence of freedom and democracy.

Cardinal Zen: In Hong Kong the situation is obviously different. We have never had persecution as in the rest of China. Here the main enemy is secularism. Despite this, our Church in Hong Kong maintains its own vitality and we have an average of 2,000 baptisms a year.

After 1997, with the return of Hong Kong to China, the situation has changed and the Church has had the duty to defend the weakest and the poor. Furthermore, it is the Church that teaches us to be concerned for the whole man; we are called to put the leaven of humanity in social relations.

Q: You have created a reputation for yourself of being hard, of openly confronting the Chinese regime without much circumlocution. Is this the right strategy to deal with Beijing?

Cardinal Zen: I have never premeditated how I will act. In fact, I have intervened strongly on two issues: the first to defend the canonization of the Chinese martyrs, held on 1 October 2000. The government invented a letter signed by all the Chinese bishops protesting this canonization. But it was false; the government knew that the vast majority of bishops did not agree. So I intervened harshly to unmask this attempt to discredit the Pope.

My other intervention was on the issue of democracy, more precisely on religious freedom. Beijing has already openly violated the 'Basic Law' [Hong Kong's mini-constitution] and has tried to hinder religious freedom. We Catholics, though a minority, have become parents of the whole people, a point of reference. This is how the demonstration was born that took half a million citizens to the streets.

Q: Do you think that China might soon be 'resigned' to open a true dialogue with the Holy See and abandon its prejudices?

Cardinal Zen: I think so. Today China sends many people abroad... Little by little, they realise that, in the rest of the world, countries have no problem accepting the Pope's naming of bishops, that this does not contradict love for the homeland or being good citizens. In this way, many problems might be surmounted.

Cuba

Population	Religions	Christian Population
11.3 million	Christians 44%[33] Atheist 37% Animist 18% Others 1%	5 million

As President Fidel Castro neared his 80th birthday in 2006, his regime remained apparently unassailable, exercising control over virtually every aspect of Cuban life. Nearly 50 years after the communist revolution, Cuba's poverty-stricken people still suffer at the hands of tight government regulation and bureaucracy, affiliated mass organisations, and the state security apparatus. US sanctions continue to blight the lives of Cubans across the island. In 1992, changes to the constitution saw references to atheism removed, a development which marked the beginning of a slight softening of government policy towards the Church. Perhaps more so than other Christians, Catholics have benefited from the improved Church–State relations. This climaxed with Pope John Paul II's visit to Cuba in January 1998, which provoked a surge in enthusiasm for the Church. Today, the general situation of the Catholic Church in Cuba remains unchanged, although in recent months, at least at a national level, the tone of the authorities towards the Catholic Church seems to have become a little more positive. Concerning Catholics, the following problems can be identified:

- Difficulties obtaining permission to purchase vehicles (which are extremely expensive) for the pastoral needs of the dioceses.
- Problems gaining authorisation to build new churches and chapels. The Church's struggle to meet the needs of growing congregations is in marked contrast to the huge civic building programmes that have been rolled out, causing major expansion to towns and cities.
- Difficulties gaining permission to repair places of worship. The problems are made worse by the high cost of building materials.
- Restrictions on new priests and religious entering Cuba and occasional difficulties in obtaining visa renewals and/or extensions.
- The State's refusal to hand back Church buildings that were nationalised in the 1960s. These include churches, chapels, presbyteries, universities and hospitals.
- Limited Church access to the media, which is controlled by the State.

Cuba – A break-through on the airwaves
Regime allows bishops to make radio broadcasts

ACN News[34]
April 2006

CHRISTIANS IN CUBA were in for a shock when they tuned in to their radios and heard a message from their bishop – the first of its kind for almost 50 years.

Bishop Emilio Aranguren of Holguín, south-east Cuba, gave an address on Palm Sunday, after an unexpected nod of approval from Cuba's Office for Religious Affairs, affiliated with the Central Committee of the Communist Party.

For generations, the Church in Cuba has had little or no access to the media and in Holguín it was the first such Easter message for 46 years.

There was more good news elsewhere in south-east Cuba where the faithful in the diocese of Bayamo-Manzanillo tuned in to Bishop Dionisio García Ibánez, who also gave a Holy Week broadcast.

Announcing the radio break-through to *Aid to the Church in Need*, Bishop Aranguren wrote: "When I visit the sick in their homes, I realise the vast majority pick up foreign radio stations in order to hear religious messages.

"It inspires their faith and helps them to face the needs that they have in their daily life. For this reason I asked the authorities to let me address the sick in order to encourage them to celebrate the great events in Christ's life."

The radio broadcasts were being interpreted as a sign that the State is easing up slightly towards the Church.

Near Guantánamo, in south-east Cuba, Catholics had watched helplessly as their Chapel of St Cecilia fell increasingly into disrepair but recently after years of resistance the government finally gave the go-ahead for the building to be renovated.

Late in 2005, just days before Christmas, the chapel was packed as Bishop Carlos Baladrón of Guantánamo-Baracoa presided at the inauguration of the rebuilt chapel. In his homily, the bishop said: "God has given a great Christmas present [to the faithful]."

Aid to the Church in Need put forward £6,500 (about US$12,000) to help with the work at St Cecilia's, which apart from the west façade, was totally rebuilt.

However, there are many other Church buildings that are still awaiting the necessary government approval before being repaired. Still more are in State control after a mass confiscation of Church property in the early 1960s.

Indications of improved State–Church relations in Cuba come amid signs of increasing interest in Christianity among the young.

Plans were put in place for youngsters from each of Cuba's 11 dioceses to attend the World Youth Day event in Cologne, in August 2005 led by Pope Benedict XVI.

Egypt

Population	Religions	Christian Population
75 million	Muslims 93.5% Christians 6% Others 0.5%	4.5 million

Egypt's constitution guarantees religious liberty, and permits all creeds and forms of worship, provided they are not in conflict with the country's constitutional and legal norms. The reality for Christians and other minorities is however very different. The authorities impose restrictions on the free exercise of any religion other than Islam, which is practised by the vast majority. Islam is the official religion of the Arab Republic of Egypt and *Shari'a* Islamic law is the primary source of legislation in Egypt. This means that every proposed change to the law is submitted to the professors at the Al-Azhar mosque and university in Cairo. For Christians and other minorities, the influence of the Al-Azhar professors is sinister because of the institution's alleged links with conservative and even fundamentalist forms of Islam. It means that laws and practices perceived to be contrary to *Shari'a* are restricted if not actually banned and explains the considerable influence of imams and sheiks in law and government.

But the situation is not all negative, as was witnessed by the newly elected parliament's decree in December 2005 to make it easier to gain permission to build and restore churches. MPs decided that such matters should be controlled by district governors without the need for approval from the executive.

January 2005: Shafik Saleh Shafik, the director of a shelter for Christian girls who have suffered trauma and violence, was arrested and sentenced following a trial in the Abbasseya quarter of Cairo. He was accused of going against the wishes of a 16-year-old girl and her parents by forcing her to receive help at the shelter. Later reports claimed that the parents had asked for help from the shelter after discovering that she was under pressure to convert to Islam. After a court trial lasting one month, Mr Shafik was sent to prison for a year.[35]

May 2005: A group of Coptic Christian men and women were imprisoned and forced to convert to Islam. The Christians' families protested in front of

30

a monastery in central Egypt in a bid to attract national and international media attention. Reports suggested that the young men were subjected to sexual abuse in order to force them to convert.

September 2005: Three young Christian women students were stabbed in the back by radical Muslims, apparently because they were not wearing veils. This attack took place at the Faculty of Medicine in El Minya, Upper Egypt.

October 2005: A spate of violence against Christians took place sparked by a DVD recording of a play held at St George's Church, Alexandria. The play was about a Christian who converts to Islam and whose sheikh orders him to burn churches and kill priests. On 19 October an Islamic extremist stabbed a religious sister in front of the church, wounding her seriously. Later, thousands of Muslims demonstrated, calling for the DVD to be banned. About 5,000 of them threw stones at the church. The police dispersed them with tear gas. A few hours later the riots continued in other parts of the city. The Al Hamra church was the target of an arson attack. A total of seven religious buildings were looted. The Isis hospital, which is run by the Coptic Christians, was ransacked, as was a pharmacy and a shop owned by Christians. The rioters clashed with the police and three people were killed. About 20 policemen were injured and six cars were set alight.

November 2005: Hany Samir Tawfik, a Coptic Christian, was released from prison in Gharbaliat, near Alexandria, after almost two and a half years in prison. He had been sentenced for trying to get political asylum after complaining of being persecuted for his faith in 2002 when he was working at the US Embassy in the Saudi capital, Riyadh. He was extradited to Egypt and sentenced to 28 months' imprisonment, after a summary trial in which he was allowed no appeal.

May 2006: The Egyptian Government was accused of failing to act after 14 Christians were stabbed in Alexandria.[36] In the attacks, one Christian was killed and more than a dozen were injured. In an effort to stem the unrest that followed, Egypt's parliament agreed to form a fact-finding committee to establish the cause of the attacks. The committee was given one month to report its findings. The committee failed to meet its deadline prompting complaints from Coptic Orthodox Metropolitan Wissa. He said: "Even if a committee does meet and even if they come out with a report, that report will not see the light of day."

India

Population	Religions	Christian Population
1.1 billion	Hindus 78.4%, Muslims 12.1%, Christians 2.3%, Animists 3.4%, Others 3.8%	25 million

Tension between religious communities in this vast and hugely populous country has intensified with the advance of Hindu fanaticism. Attacks on Christian communities have increased and animosity has grown between the Hindu majority and the Muslim minority. Key to the problem are the Hindu nationalist Bharatiya Janata Party (BJP), India's largest political party, and the Rashtriya Swayamsevak Sangh (RSS), a paramilitary formation of Hindu extremists that is regarded as the armed wing of the BJP. Since 2004, they have unleashed a campaign of intimidation and a 're-birth of national pride' in a bid to secure control of India's individual states. Their success means they are forcing ethnic and religious minorities to yield to an atmosphere of violence and threat.

Particularly at risk are the Dalits, perceived as the dregs of society in India's rigid caste system. A disproportionately high percentage of Dalits are Christians, causing the distinction between religion and social status to blur in the minds of Hindu extremists who subject them to oppression almost on a daily basis. This background explains statistics showing that in 2005 there were 200 attacks against Catholics alone.[37]

According to many government critics, the problems are compounded by new laws which are seen as making the oppression of minorities an essential component of government. A number of states across India have introduced legislation banning religious conversions. Critics say the laws make accusations of apostasy very easy to argue and institutionalise an attitude of suspicion towards minorities.

August 2005: The Vishwa Hindu Parishad (VHP), paramilitary Hindu extremists, called for an inquiry into the funds from abroad given to Christian missionaries. The *Daily Dharitri*, the most widely read daily newspaper in the Indian state of Orissa, carried a report that in the previous three years the Church received about 4.5 billion rupees (US$95 million) to "finance conversion activities in the country".[38] No reference was made to the funds received by Hindus and Muslims. In an interview, Archbishop Raphael Cheenath of Cuttack and Bhubaneshwar declared: "This strategy is orchestrated by the VHP in order to compromise the charitable agencies and the Christian missions. It is a sinister plan... If you want to find out what funds are given to Hindu agencies, you have to contact the Department of Finance; yet the funds given to Christians are printed in detail on the front pages of the newspapers." He continued: "The VHP is planning a *Dharma Sansad*, [religious gathering] in the famous Hindu place of pilgrimage in the district of Puri in the state of Orissa. They intend to use this meeting to mobilise public support for their cause against the Christian missionaries, with the tacit support of the government, which is doing nothing to stop them or their activities."

September 2005: Fr Agnos Bara, assistant priest of Baba Bira, in the state of Jharkhand, was murdered while trying to calm a disturbance involving tribal Christians who were under attack from Hindu extremists. Fr Anand Jojo, vicar general of the local diocese, said: "Behind the assassination of this priest can be seen the hand of the forces of the extreme right. These people are acting with the tacit support of the government and have created all sorts of problems in the area."[39] Cardinal Telesphore Toppo, President of India's Catholic bishops' conference, described Fr Agnos as "a martyr of peace".

October 2005: Five sisters of the Congregation of the Virgins of the Lord were beaten while waiting for a bus in Bhandaria, a town in the western state of Rajasthan. One sister, Mother Rosario, 68, was gravely injured, while all the others had minor injuries. Bishop Joseph Pathalil of Udaipur commented: "These noble sisters only want to do their best for the local population, but this is precisely what the fundamentalists do not want. They [the fundamentalists] enjoy the tacit protection of the government and nobody is able to stop them."

November 2005: The President of the All India Catholic Union (AICU) sent a letter to Prime Minister Manmohan Singh recalling the many times he had written in the past about how states controlled by the BJP had "State machinery stained with violence".[40] He said that in states such as Rajasthan, Madhya Pradesh and Gujarat, the BJP's policy "seems designed to block the efforts of the Christian community in its campaign for equality of rights for the Christian dalits". He called on the government to produce a document about the situation for Christians.

April 2006: A law banning so-called forced conversions was passed by the state of Rajasthan in west India.[41] Under the legislation, those found guilty of converting by allurement, greed or intimidation were liable to prison terms of up to five years. Then in a dramatic development, Pratibha Patil, the Governor of Rajasthan state, came down against the legislation, apparently after receiving complaints from religious minorities.[42] The BJP-led government in the state said his intervention was unconstitutional. The law coincided with Hindu claims of Christian missionaries carrying out forced conversions in the town of Kota. But opposition congress leaders joined religious groups including Christians in opposing the law, saying it paved the way for government-sponsored intimidation of minorities. Other Indian states which have passed anti-conversion laws include Gujarat, Tamil Nadu, Madhya Pradesh and Orissa. Hindu nationalists have openly said the laws are aimed at Christian evangelicals. In response, Christian communities have spoken of the harassment suffered by the faithful who face questioning from police officials who ask them to justify their faith and to explain why they are not Hindus. Christian leaders have reported how nuns and priests are asked about the source of their funding, why they have come to the state and the number of people who have converted under their influence.[43]

June 2006: Extremists dragged an independent Christian pastor to a police station in Karnataka state, accusing him of converting Hindus to Christianity.[44] They beat Pastor Sundar Rao severely both inside the police station and after he was released. The pastor has since been hospitalised. A local Christian, who requested anonymity, said the police were mute spectators to the beatings. The Christian said: "The extremists forced Rao to sign a piece of blank paper inside the police station. They also told him the land he had bought for a church would instead be used for constructing a temple."

Indonesia (and East Timor)

Population	Religions	Christian Population
225 million	Muslims 55%, New religions 22%, Christians 13%, Hindus 3%, Others 7%	29 million

Terrorism and Islamic extremism as well as political in-fighting represent a threat to religious liberty in certain regions of Indonesia. Pressure from Islamic extremists has, from time to time, forced churches to close and prevented new ones from being built. In response, the authorities have reviewed the rules governing the construction of religious buildings. People in the Poso region remain nervous after continuing violence including murders and hand-bombs. The authorities are being criticised for not doing enough to catch those responsible.

A number of Christians are in prison, among them three Catholics in Palu awaiting execution following a court case prompted by accusations made by Islamic extremists. The allegations are denied by Christian religious leaders and human rights activists. Christians are not alone in facing oppression. Extremists are demanding followers of the Ahmadi religion be banned from practising their faith, not least because they do not recognise Mohammed as the last Prophet.

But, as in many Islamic countries, Christians are increasingly at risk from highly-motivated and well organised Muslim extremists, such as the men responsible for October 2002's Bali bomb, which killed 202 people. At the end of 2005, public security forces from the Indonesian capital, Jakarta, warned that at least 3,000 Indonesians were ready and willing to carry out terrorist attacks across the region. These *Jihad* warriors were allegedly veterans of conflicts in Libya, Afghanistan and the Philippines, working out of Java, Sumatra and Sulawesi. This news coincided with reports that Indonesian security forces were on red alert after uncovering a vast terrorist plan targeting Catholic churches and other public buildings over the Christmas period.

August 2005: Two hundred Islamic extremists forced the closure of the Catholic chapel of Margahayu, near Buah Batu, in West Java province. At the end of the afternoon Mass, the group approached the priest and

35

demanded the immediate closure of the chapel. Desperate to prevent the faithful from being beaten up, the parish priest gave in to their demands. By the time the provincial authorities arrived, the fundamentalists had long since departed. The authorities offered their apologies.

October 2005: Construction of a new church in the district of Bekasi, West Java, was halted after pressure from as many as nine fundamentalist Muslim organisations.[45] The authorities gave in to the demands despite the local Christian community meeting all the criteria needed for permission to build the church. It followed an incident the previous month (September 2005) in which 500 people demonstrated against the church, shouting violent anti-Christian slogans. About 200 of them returned to demonstrate again ten days later. On 3 October another protest was held on the site of the future church. The demonstrators shouted: "Not a single church must be built here!"

October 2005: A group of Catholics were attacked while reciting the rosary in a private house in West Jakarta. The attackers forced them to stop praying to Our Lady and then demanded that the faithful sign a declaration promising not to pray again in their homes.

December 2005: Indonesian security forces were put on a state of alert after discovering a terrorist plan to target Catholic churches over Christmas. Reports said that behind the attacks was an Islamist called Azahari, an expert in bomb-making and a member of the *Jemaah Islamiya* militant group. He was also suspected of being responsible for the attacks in Bali in 2002 and 2005. The intended targets were the Catholic churches in Malang, a tourist region about 50 miles south of Surabaya, the capital of East Java. Malang is well known as a Catholic centre with many religious orders such as the Divine Word Missionaries and the Carmelites. There is also a major seminary at Malang, attended by hundreds of students for the priesthood and religious novices. In the months leading up to Christmas, the police imposed blanket controls throughout the country, "to prevent attacks against the churches". Checkpoints were set up along main roads and village leaders were asked to notify police of any suspect behaviour.

December 2005: An anonymous message sent to the radio station *Timor Voice* announced: "On the eve of the New Year, 31 churches in Kupang [in the province of East Nusa Tenggara] will suffer the same fate as Bali with the bombs in October. From the head of the *Jemaah Islamiya* of the Eastern region. The *Jihad* for the Prophet Mohammed." This threat was considered to be "serious" and imminent by the local head of police. The security forces drafted into the area 2,500 men, both police and soldiers, and ordered a round-the-clock surveillance of all churches. Subsequently, ACN received no reports of incidents against Christians.

Early 2006: According to the Communications Forum of the Churches in the province of West Java, Islamic fundamentalists forcibly closed a total of 35 churches in the area during 2005. The forum reported on an escalation in violence and threats against 'illegal' churches, beginning in the middle of 2004.

May 2006: Police in Indonesia announced that seven suspected Islamic terrorists had confessed to beheading three Indonesian schoolgirls in Poso, on the Indonesian island of Sulawesi, in October 2005.[46] Theresia Morangke, 15, Alfita Poliwo, 17, and Yarni Sambue, 15 were beheaded early in the morning of 29 October 2005 as they walked to a Christian school in Poso district. A fourth girl, Noviana Malewa, 15, received serious injuries to her face and neck but survived the attack. Five men were arrested on 5 May in central Sulawesi. *The Jakarta Post* identified them as Apriyantono, alias Irwan; Arman, alias Haris; Asrudin; Nano; and Abdul Muis. "Two of the arrested men were involved in the murders", national police spokesman Brig Gen Anton Bachrul Alam told reporters. "Another was detained for carrying ammunition, while the other two were arrested as accessories to the crimes." Two additional suspects have not yet been publicly identified.

Iran

Population	Religions	Christian Population
70.7 million	Muslims 95.6% Zoroastrians 2.8% Christians 0.3% Others 1.3%	200,000

The victory of the radical outsider Mahmoud Ahmadinejad in the Iranian elections of August 2005 sparked fears of a return to the most repressive days of Islamic leader Ayatollah Khomeini. The new president has already signalled his determination to raise the profile of Islam in defiance of the USA and Israel. As the world's main *Shi'a* Muslim nation, governed by conservative clerics, the outlook for religious minorities is bleak. Mr Ahmadinejad's religious tolerance credentials would seem to be in tatters after his sensational claim that the holocaust was "myth" and that Israel "should be wiped off the map". A new radicalism in Iranian politics could well hit Christians hard after years of setbacks. Within just 30 years, the number of Christians has fallen by up to two-thirds with many emigrating to the West. Up to half of the foreign clergy were forced to leave in the immediate aftermath of Ayatollah Khomeini's rise to power in 1979. Since then clergy numbers have slumped still further. Although Christian worship is permitted, Christians are treated as second class citizens and have had to suffer the humiliations that come with living in an Islamic state where *Shari'a* law is in place.

2005: The Chaldean Archbishop of Teheran, the Iranian capital, gave an interview in which he explained the decline in the Christian population. Archbishop Ramzi Garmou said the fall in numbers "is partly due to a birth rate that is lower among the Christians, but above all due to emigration, which has accelerated since the Islamic revolution and the war against Iraq." He continued: "Obviously there are also human, cultural, socio-economic and historical aspects at the root of such a phenomenon. But the fact that the Christians belong to minorities that are distinguished not only by their religious faith but also by their language and culture has made them doubly strangers in the eyes of the people."[47]

February 2005: The case against Hamid Pourmand, who was accused of 'military espionage', was dropped and instead he was charged with 'proselytism' and 'apostasy'. Dismissed from his post as colonel in the Army, the Iranian was lucky to escape the death penalty. Three months later, on 28 May, the charges were dismissed by an Islamic judge who reportedly said: "I don't know who you are but the rest of the world does." He was referring to the international campaign to get him released. Afterwards, Mr Pourmand was still in prison but the authorities gave him permission to see his family for three days a month in recognition of his good conduct.

November 2005: Another Iranian, Ghorban Tori, aged 50, who had converted to Christianity in Turkmenistan before returning to Iran, was abducted at his home. Hours later, his body was found in front of his house. He had been beaten to death. He ran an independent Protestant church, composed essentially of Muslim converts, and had received threats in the months before his death.

May 2006: An Iranian Christian who converted from Islam 33 years ago was placed under arrest and interrogation in northern Iran, where secret police held him incommunicado. Ali Kaboli, 51, was taken into custody on 2 May from his workshop in Gorgan, capital of Iran's northern province of Golestan.[48] To date no charges have been filed against Kaboli, who has been threatened in the past with legal prosecution for holding 'illegal' religious meetings in his home. He could also be charged for converting to Christianity, which under Iran's apostasy laws is punishable by death. "Everyone knew that his house was under control [police surveillance] for many years," an Iranian Christian now living abroad said. "They even pushed him to leave the country about three years ago, but he told them he preferred to stay inside the country, even if it meant living in an Iranian jail."

Iraq

Population	Religions	Christian Population
20 million	*Shi'a* Muslim 60%	700,000
	Sunni Muslim 36%	
	Christians, 3.5%	
	Others 0.5%	

Hopes have quickly begun to fade that peace will be restored, even after the sweeping political and administrative developments of 2005–6. Key wording in the permanent constitution prompted Christian leaders to fear that the country was set to become an Islamic state, with the attendant problem of institutionalised discrimination against minorities, especially Christians. The elections of December 2005 held out little promise of significant representation of Christians in Parliament as hard-line *Shi'a* Muslims brokered a deal with Kurds to secure the necessary majority. But worse than the many setbacks in the country's newly-emerging national administration has been the apparently endless cycle of violence engulfing significant parts of the country. With little sign of an immediate end to the bloodshed, a state of turmoil has been fuelled by the increasing conflict between *Shi'a* and *Sunni* Muslims, both of which have come under the growing influence of militants. The escalation of violence was not thought to end with the death in June 2006 of Abu Musab al-Zarqawi, Iraq's self-appointed Al Qaeda leader. The *Sunni–Shi'a* clash is exacerbated by the fact that although the *Sunni* Muslims are a minority, they are concentrated in large numbers in key areas of the country. Perhaps more so than other groups – especially minorities – Christians have been living in fear of their lives with many reports of killings, kidnappings and attacks on churches and other properties. Christians, who enjoyed certain levels of protection under Saddam Hussein, have fled in vast numbers to Syria, Jordan, Turkey and other countries. The Christian population, which was about one million before 2003, has now plummeted to about 700,000. Reports have indicated that Iraq's Christians are falsely seen as secret sympathisers with the American-led forces, who are perceived as latter-day 'crusaders'. In a country where Christianity traces its origins back to the 1st Century AD, the crisis threatening the Church is felt all the more keenly because of its long and glorious history.

January 2005: Syrian Catholic Archbishop Basile Georges Casmoussa of Mosul was kidnapped after visiting a family of parishioners in the city.[49] He was confronted at gunpoint and bundled into a car. Next day he was released. Initial reports, later disputed, suggested that a US$200,000 ransom was requested by his kidnappers. Reports suggested that the kidnapping was politically motivated and was aimed at discouraging Christians from taking part in up-coming elections at the end of the month. ACN reports said it was a revenge attack following the archbishop's refusal to comply with Arab demands for Christians to leave the city and the surrounding villages. The incident came barely a month after the Chaldean Archbishop Faraj Rahho of Mosul was frogmarched out of his home by masked men who torched the building.[50] In a message to ACN, a Baghdad priest wrote: "Pray for us and especially for Archbishop Rahho. Both he and the priests are very shaken. The archbishop just had to stand in front of his home and watch it burn."

January 2005: The Secretary General of the Christian Democratic Party of Iraq, Minas Ibrahim al Yussufi, was kidnapped. The kidnappers, who did not reveal their identity, demanded the withdrawal of the Americans.

January 2005: Elections were held following a campaign of intimidation against the Christian political parties. Reports suggested they were forbidden to wear crosses or depict crosses on election literature.

February 2005: *Shi'a* victory at the polls prompted fears of *Shari'a* law being introduced. Only six Christians were elected to the new parliament.

March 2005: Islamist group the 'Brigades for the elimination of Christian agents and spies' announced a witch-hunt of Christians accused of collaborating with the US-led forces "right into their homes and churches".

May 2005: On a visit to France, Emmanuel III Delly, Patriarch of Baghdad of the Chaldeans, declared: "Religious liberty does not exist in Muslim countries, with the exception of Lebanon... In Iraq, there is ... no religious liberty – nor is there any political or cultural liberty."

August and September 2005: Christian leaders in Iraq spoke out after the appearance of a new draft of the country's constitution which stated: "No law can be passed that contradicts the undisputed rules of Islam" (Clause 2(a)).[51] After a meeting of Chaldean bishops, Patriarch Emmanuel III Delly declared that the constitution "opens the door" to the discrimination of

Christians. Bishop Andreas Abouna of Baghdad asked for help from Cardinal Cormac Murphy-O'Connor, Archbishop of Westminster. He told the cardinal that unless a dramatic intervention took place, the constitution could pave the way for the country to be turned into an Islamic state with huge restrictions for minority groups. The cardinal responded by writing to British Foreign Secretary Jack Straw, asking for Clause 2(a) to be withdrawn from the constitution and warning of "a Christian exodus from Iraq". He called on the Foreign Secretary to include in the constitution "specific guarantees which establish the equality of non-Muslims." ACN UK National Director Neville Kyrke-Smith spoke of the "threat of *Shari'a* coming through via the back door". A later message from the Foreign Secretary to the cardinal acknowledged the severity of the problem but urged optimism for the future of Iraq's Christian community.

October 2005: The Permanent Constitution was ratified with a huge majority vote. Concerns about the place of Islam and *Shari'a* were still unresolved.

October 2005: Two key Christian leaders from Baghdad held a meeting at London's Houses of Parliament to reveal the growing crisis for Christians in Iraq.[52] Canon Andrew White, from St George's (Church of England) Church, Baghdad, described how there was "a price on my head" and that it was now unsafe for him to make the short journey from his home to church for services. Canon White said all the lay-leaders at his church suddenly disappeared and had presumably been kidnapped. He said a close associate of the church had also disappeared with a ransom requested for his release. When his loved ones paid the ransom, the man was killed and his head was sent to his relatives and friends in a bag. Yonadam Kanna, General Secretary of the Assyrian Democratic Movement, Iraq's largest Christian party, said that mass emigration had left Christian villages up to 50 percent empty. He said people leaving had given their house keys to neighbours only to discover within a few weeks that the neighbours had also left. He said "People are worried that things are getting worse and worse."

November 2005: Iraq President Jalal Talabani told Pope Benedict XVI that the new Iraq constitution would respect Christians and other minority religious groups.[53] The Vatican had expressed concern that a legal system drawing on Islamic *Shari'a* might undermine the rights of Christians. Mr Talabani was reported as saying: "I explained to His Holiness that the Iraqi constitution will consider all Iraqis, Christians included."

January 2006: *Shi'a* Muslims emerged victorious in December 2005's General Elections and brokered a deal with the Kurds, the second largest party.[54] Concerns grew that the *Shi'a* Muslims would turn Iraq into a theocratic state. Bishop Abouna of Iraq said: "We need to speak up now otherwise it could mean we lose the future for Christianity in the area." The bishop also expressed concern about widespread reports of electoral fraud.

January 2006: At least three people died and more than 20 people were injured when bombers in Iraq targeted six churches packed with people.[55] Parishioners ran for their lives after car-bombers struck in co-ordinated attacks that took place as Sunday services got under way in Baghdad and the northern city of Kirkuk. In the capital, Emmanuel III Delly, Patriarch of Baghdad of the Chaldeans, narrowly escaped with his life. Archbishop Louis Sako of Kirkuk said Iraq's Christians were "becoming once again a Church of martyrs".[56] He spoke just hours after conducting the funeral of 14-year-old Fadi Raad Elias, who died in the bomb blast. Fadi, an altar server, had been preparing for Mass at Kirkuk's Church of the Immaculate Child when a bomb went off. Elsewhere in Baghdad and also in the northern city of Mosul, dozens of Christian university students were physically attacked by Muslim undergraduates who shouted slogans against them, calling them non-believers and American agents.

March 2006: Baghdad Bishop Andreas Abouna gave his bleakest assessment yet of the situation for Iraqi Christians, saying many were living in fear of their lives.[57] "The Christians feel desperate and so many are leaving." He added: "In their hearts they do not want to leave their country, but because of the situation, they prefer to be outside Iraq." It came as Emmanuel III Delly, Patriarch of Baghdad of the Chaldeans, called for a two-day fast for peace. "We have moved away from piety and virtue," he said. "Because of this, the blood of so many brothers has been shed and so many children have become orphans."[58]

June 2006: Baghdad priest, Fr Jamil Nissan, narrowly escaped death after a bomb smashed the wall at his Church of the Ascension, in Baghdad.[59] The church hall was damaged but nobody was hurt. Parishioners spent the night with the priest to calm his nerves. Bishop Abouna of Baghdad said: "When the people were told about the attack on the church, they ... knew the priest would feel very alone. They knew that as a human being he would be very afraid. They wanted to stay with him." He added: "Of course people are frightened – but there is something stronger than their fear, it is their faith."

Interview with Archbishop Louis Sako of Kirkuk

ACN UK, published in *The Catholic Times*
June 2004

ARCHBISHOP LOUIS SAKO has a claim to fame few can match – he confronted Saddam Hussein face to face. The extraordinary incident happened when the then Fr Sako made plans to return to his native Iraq after completing a doctorate in Rome.

The Saddam government refused to recognise his qualification and prevented him from returning home where he intended to start teaching. Such a bombshell would have stunned most people into silence but Louis Sako is different. If he was angered and upset, Louis Sako did not let his feelings get the better of him.

Instead, he demanded to see President Saddam Hussein in person. Astonishingly, the request was granted and soon he was whisked off to one of Saddam's palaces. The sight of Saddam shocked him to the core. "He is not like you see him on television at all," said an animated Archbishop Sako as he recalled the incident, which took place many years ago. "In public he wears a lot of make-up. When I saw him, he seemed just like an old sheik, his face all wrinkly – but he was very, very tough."

Ruthless, maybe, but the archbishop also recalls Saddam as displaying a kindly streak. "He told me: 'God bless you – please pray for me'." Then it was down to business: "I presented my problem to him and told him it was my right to go back and help my people."

Saddam told his visitor to wait and an answer would come "in a month or so". But – shock horror – a letter soon came through once again rejecting his application. Undaunted, the then Fr Sako began studying for another doctorate. This time, luck was on his side - the government recognition came through because his subject – Roman/Persian cultural exchange – had precious little religious content.

A steely nerve quickly emerges as one of Louis Sako's strongest traits – a characteristic sorely needed as he treads a precarious path in a country deep in crisis. The problems are many – few priests, he has only four in his Kirkuk diocese in northern Iraq, churches are few and far between and there are fears that Iraq's massive Muslim majority will turn as militant as its Iranian and Saudi Arabian neighbours.

But perhaps the biggest worry is the emigration of Christians from Iraq and the Middle East – a phenomenon that amounts to little less than a mass exodus. In Iraq alone, Archbishop Sako maintains that thousands leave the country every year.

Now Iraq's total Christian population is about 700,000, barely half what it was at the start of 2003. Why are they leaving? Iraq's security crisis combined with the Americans' decision to open up the country's borders means that the people see little or no Christian presence in a land where the Church once thrived.

It is an ancient civilization, which holds some of Christianity's oldest and most revered cultural icons, many of them now reduced to dust. Half the country was Christian when the Muslims first made their presence felt in the early seventh century.

"We must encourage the Christian communities to stay in Iraq," said Archbishop Sako emphatically. "Yes, the security situation is bad but I am very optimistic about the future." Stressing the "liberal" nature of Iraqi Islam, he speaks of the "conviviality" of relations between Christians and Muslims and the growth of Christian parties and magazines since the overthrow of Saddam.

Archbishop Sako is determined that the good relations existing between Muslims and Christians for centuries should be strengthened wherever possible. He has devised badly needed projects to help the poor and the sick in a way that cuts across the religious divide. He has set up vital support schemes to poverty-stricken families – foster-homes, food and clothing – all backed by emergency aid funding from *Aid to the Church in Need*, the Catholic charity, which supports persecuted and oppressed Christians.

Archbishop Sako wants to build on these foundations with new hospitals, medical dispensaries, youth centres and women's groups. He has plans to set up computer courses, launch new magazines and set up programmes teaching people vocational skills such as farming.

Christians setting a good example of positive social action is key to the archbishop's vision of the Church. He said: "If we want to be a strong

Church, we have to be different from the Muslims. We have to be strong enough to speak up when it is necessary to do so. We have to teach the Muslims a new theological language in which they don't look at everything as pre-destined by God, and completely beyond the control of human beings. We need to show them that we as a society must work for the improvement of human rights, of the value of the individual. We must not be people motivated by revenge."

By nature a man of rigorous intellectual independence, Archbishop Sako said it was only right that the Church had to reform itself before encouraging Muslims to do the same. "There are too many churches in our part of the world – there's us, the Chaldeans, the Assyrians, the Latin-rite, the Orthodox. If we stay as we are, we will have no future. We are already losing ground. We need to reform ourselves at all levels – human, pastoral, religious and canonic."

As he struggles to repair the few churches in his diocese, the immediate concern is to find something better than a few plastic chairs to provide seating in a chapel not far outside Kirkuk.

With churches being bombed, Christians emigrating and the country becoming ensnared in a bloody conflict between *Sunni* and *Shi'a* Muslims, a tendency towards despair would be understandable at the very least. Not so, the upbeat Archbishop Sako. After all, this is a man who took his problem direct to Saddam Hussein and who – against all the odds – triumphed.

Israel/Palestine

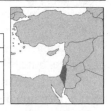

	Israel	Palestine
Population	6.7 million	3.8 million
Major religions	Judaism	Islam
	Islam	
Christian population	1.8 % (190,000)	

Pressures from all sides – political, social and religious – have proved unbearable for thousands upon thousands of Christians in the Holy Land who have reluctantly fled the place of Christ's birth in increasing numbers. In 2005, reports revealed that the proportion of Christians had plummeted from 20 percent to less than two percent within just 40 years. In 2005 and 2006, Christians in the region received twin blows that were set only to increase the rate of emigration. Israel's erection of a barrier along the Palestinian borders further embittered already strained relations with Christians who have long since felt oppressed and discriminated against at the hands of the Israeli authorities. If the barrier was a setback for minority Christians in Israel, for their co-religionists in Palestine it was little short of disastrous. Largely prevented from getting through the barrier, many of them were in effect completely cut off from jobs, health care and education – all to be found in Israel. The problem affected Palestinians as a whole but for the Christians the set-back became a crisis with the election of militant group Hamas, who many believed would set about an Islamisation of politics and society, creating a culture inherently hostile to non-Muslims. Concern turned to alarm and even despair in the summer of 2006 when hostilities broke out between Israel and Lebanon-based militants, Hezbollah. Church leaders and activists for minorities in the Holy Land stepped up demands for the West to pay heed to the growing problems engulfing the region's Christian communities, urging prayer and action to keep hope alive.

2005: A detailed analysis of Christians in Palestine from 1992 to 2004 was produced by Professor Justus Reid Weiner of the Hebrew University of Jerusalem.[60] Professor Weiner wrote: "The radicalisation of the Palestinian Islamic communities living under the Palestinian National Authority is developing into a dangerous threat to the Christian communities, to the individuals and the lifestyle they practice. The return towards the archaic and fundamentalist ideology supported by the fundamentalist Muslims,

47

aggravated by the difficult economic and social conditions, has ... caused a high rate of emigration among the Christians from the Middle East. The Palestinian Christian community is not only faced with a threat to its very existence, but still more significantly, its status as a persecuted minority is overlooked, because international attention is focused on terrorism and its own embryonic plans for peace, rather than on the present needs of human rights."

February 2005: About 5,000 Christians fled for their lives after being targeted by fanatic members of the Druze, an Islamic sect, who went on the rampage in the Israeli town of Maghar, ten miles north-west of the Sea of Galilee. Up to 4,000 people attacked the Christians with bottles, petrol bombs and stones. About 125 shops and homes were damaged and about 180 cars were burned.[61] When the Christians tried to resist the attackers they were beaten up.[62] Don Ronen, the Israeli Government's northern district commissioner, called the attack "a pogrom". Greek Catholic priest Fr Maher Aboud eventually persuaded most of the Christian families to return to their damaged homes and Sunday Mass attendance soon swelled to 800 in his Church of St George. The police were severely criticised for reported failure to restore law and order until the attacks had entered their third day. The head of the committee for internal affairs of the Knesset, Raleb Majadele, deplored the lack of intervention by the police during the violence. "It is intolerable that the police ... did not do anything." Fr Aboud described the shock for the Christian community, which represents 50 percent of the town's 18,000 population. He said: "We have been looking and looking to find what we could have done to deserve this and we can find nothing. Reports claimed that the incident had been sparked by rumours that Christians were responsible for a picture of the head of a Druze girl pasted onto an image of a naked body. The allegation was sharply refuted by counter-claims that Druze had been behind the offending picture.

May 2005: Marie-Ange Siebrecht, head of ACN's Asia–Africa Projects Desk, returned from a trip to the Holy Land with reports of a worsening state of affairs for Christians in key parts of Palestine.[63] "The situation in the Holy Land is really depressing, above all because of the terrible war that is totally separating the Palestinian territories from Israel. Bethlehem has been transformed into a place that is extremely difficult for the Christians." She added: "Christians are particularly hard hit by the present situation because they cannot gain access to their places of work in Israel. In places like Bethlehem, there are practically no tourists anymore, owing to the tension in the region."

Other reports from the trip also revealed bad treatment of Christians by the Israeli authorities, including institutionalised anti-Christian sentiment in the police force.[64]

September 2005: Shouting "Allah Akbar" (God is great) and "Burn the Crusaders", Muslim aggressors set fire to homes, shops, and a petrol station in an attack on Christians in the village of Taybeh, north-west of Ramallah, in the West Bank.[65] The incident was sparked by rumours of a relationship developing between a 23-year-old woman and the son of her Christian employer, who lived in Taybeh. The woman, called Hiyam Ajaj, was murdered by her own family who then turned on Taybeh. A woman living in one of the houses destroyed in Taybeh, said: "They did this because we are Christians. They did so because we are the weakest."[66]

September 2005: A dossier of 93 alleged incidents of abuse by "Islamic fundamentalist media" against Palestinian Christians was presented to Church leaders in Jerusalem. The document, put together by Christians in the Holy Land, listed 140 cases of apparent land theft. According to the report, Christians in the West Bank were allegedly forced off their land by gangs backed by corrupt judicial officials. The media said the dossier showed the Church was breaking its "self-imposed silence" after years of work not to upset the delicate ethnic and social sectarian balance in the region. Fr Pierbattista Pizzaballa, the custodian of the Holy Land, said: "The Christian community has always suffered in the last few years because we are a minority. Many have the temptation to leave, so the community is shrinking." While he stressed that "we are not talking about a confrontation with all Muslims", he added: "We don't want to see violations of the law – sometimes we have to raise our voices."[67] The alleged attacks on Christians have come despite repeated appeals to the Palestinian Authority to rein in Muslim gangs.

November 2005: At a meeting with Israeli President Moshe Katzav, Pope Benedict XVI requested that Israel give legal recognition to the Catholic Church in Israel. According to Church sources, Israel agreed a plan to give recognition to Church institutions in Israel as part of a series of "agreements" reached with the Holy See in the 1990s. The Israeli Government recently informed the Supreme Court of Israel that it does not recognise its obligations under this agreement. If the Church is granted the required legal status, it would be granted access to civil courts to protect its buildings and reclaim other properties confiscated over the years.

December 2005: The Mayor of Bethlehem, Victor Batarseh, criticised the Palestinian National Authority for failing to provide the city with enough funds to prepare for the Christmas festivities. He went on to lambaste the Israeli authorities for creating an "oppressive" atmosphere caused by new checkpoints around the city. Mr Batarseh, a Catholic, told *Asia News*: "Israel is waging an economic war on Bethlehem because they know that we depend on tourism from the pilgrims."[68] He said security checks by police for people accessing the city had got "slower and slower". The Mayor sent messages to Christian leaders in Jerusalem and around the world, calling on them to lobby the Israeli authorities to "soften the controls and secure a greater influx of faithful."

January 2006: Concerns were raised about the prospects for Christians in the Palestinian territories after the election of the militant resistance movement, Hamas. Christians in the territories described their fears about the possible re-introduction of the *jizya*, a tax originally derived from the *Qur'an* to be paid by infidels – non-Muslims. The fears of *jizya* centred on Bethlehem too, after militants took control of the city following the election of Hamas. In a report in the Wall Street Journal, Hassan El Masalmeh said: "We of Hamas will one day or another introduce this tax."[69]

March 2006: Life has turned "from bad to worse" since the election of Hamas, according to an inside report on the situation for Christians in the West Bank.[70] Minority Christian communities already under threat from increasing tension between Palestinians and the Israelis have told of a collapse in confidence resulting from a dramatic shift towards radicalism under the new Islamist Hamas regime. Describing the "terrible pressures" on the Christian community, Catholics in Bethlehem faced worsening problems including the international freeze on donations to the Palestinian authority, more security problems, and increased travel restrictions caused by the controversial barrier separating Israel from the West Bank. With a squeeze on public finances and frequent problems travelling to Jerusalem where many Palestinians work and shop, the crisis for the area's 190,000 Christians has deepened, especially with increased intolerance of non-Muslims since Hamas's election in January. A shopkeeper, who sells Christian devotional gifts in Bethlehem, said: "It has become awful living

50

here." The Palestinian Christian, who cannot be named for security reasons, added: "We do not believe what is happening. Since the election, things have been getting worse and worse." He said access to Jerusalem was frequently impossible with Israeli authorities closing the roads, preventing access to Tel Aviv Airport and the city centre, where many Palestinians work. He said: "Every second day it seems, you cannot get through the barrier from here to Israel. How can we survive? Everything here is in the hands of the Israelis and without them we cannot do anything." The shopkeeper stressed the importance of a scheme masterminded by *Aid to the Church in Need* which is generating funds for Christians in the West Bank by retailing their hand-made olive wood devotional items including crucifixes, cribs and rosaries.

June 2006: Pope Benedict XVI spoke of his distress concerning the plight of Christians in the Holy Land.[71] Speaking to a meeting of organisations funding Eastern Churches at the Vatican Congregation for Oriental Churches (ROACO), the Pope said: "The serious difficulties [they are] going though because of profound insecurity, lack of work, innumerable restrictions and … growing poverty are a cause of pain for us all. It is a situation that makes the educational, professional and family future of young generations extremely uncertain. [It] tempts them to leave forever the beloved land of their birth. Our prime and fundamental duty is that of persistent and faithful prayer to the Lord, who never abandons his children in times of trial. This should be associated with activities of fraternal [support], in order to find new and at times unexpected ways to meet the needs of those people."

Laos

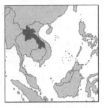

Population	Religions	Christian Population
6.3 million	Buddhist 60% Christian 1.5% Other 38.5%	100,000

The constitution of 1991 guarantees religious freedom under Article 30 but the reality of life in Laos is very different. Greater tolerance in the last 15 years has paved the way for the re-opening of churches and temples but religious practice is still only possible within limits imposed by the socialist regime. Under Decree 92 promulgated in 2002, the government reserves the right to interfere in religious practice on the pretext of enforcing law and order. As a result, grave violations of human rights and religious liberty continue to take place. Under particular threat are ethnic minorities groups, some of whom are converting to Christianity.

March 2005: After 30 years, a new church was finally opened in the north of Laos. The Church of Our Lady of Fatima in Ban Pong Vang was consecrated by the Apostolic Nuncio to Laos, Archbishop Salvatore Pennacchio. Leading the Easter liturgies at the church was Monsignor Thopahang, who was repeatedly imprisoned by the State, most recently in 1998.

Since July 2005, at least 6,000 refugees were caught in a diplomatic row between Laos and its neighbour, Thailand. The Thai government wants to repatriate the refugees but they have refused, complaining bitterly about the lack of human rights. The Laos government does not want the refugees to return. The Laos regime is particularly opposed to the repatriation of those among the refugees who are Christian. The government dismisses Christianity as alien to the Laotian way of life and a "foreign imperialist religion" heavily influenced by the political agenda of the West, especially the USA.

December 2005: The government dramatically intervened at the last minute to prevent the ordination of Sophone Vilavongsy, 32, Laotian and Oblate Missionary of Mary Immaculate. It was to have been Laos's first ordination to the priesthood in 30 years. Reports say the government had initially given the ordination the go-ahead on condition the ceremony was not held in public.[72] The last Laotian Oblate to be ordained, Monsignor J. Khamse Vithavong, the apostolic vicar of Vientiane, reported that soldiers kept guard around the church to prevent the ordination from going ahead. No reason was given for stopping the ceremony. This priest was ordained on 18 June.[73]

2005: A group of Christians belonging to the Bru ethnic group were arrested in southern Laos before being tortured in an attempt to force them to deny their faith. Reports say the group of up to 24 were jailed in Muang Phine prison and were beaten, chained and were tortured with red ants. They were forced to sign a document renouncing their faith, and those who did so were released. Two, however, refused to sign and were imprisoned for three years. The authorities alleged that they had "possessed illegal arms", a claim denied by the Laotian Movement for Human Rights, based in Paris.[74]

Nigeria

Population	Religions	Christian Population
130 million	Christians 45.9% Muslims 43.9% Animists 9.8% Others 0.4%	59.7 million

The events of early 2006 made all too clear the sharp divisions opening up in Africa's most populous country. Lurching from one dictatorship to another, Nigeria is now perilously close to breaking apart along religious and ethnic lines. Concerns over the spread of militant Islam have grown with as many as 12 States in Nigeria – one-third of the total – now under some form of *Shari'a* Islamic law. The automatic discrimination and even persecution of non-Muslims that is an essential part of *Shari'a* have led to widespread displacement of Christian communities. The response from many Christian communities has been to deepen their faith and Nigeria boasts up to 7,000 seminarians. But the breakdown in relations, compounded by issues of poverty and unemployment, meant that clashes between Muslims and Christians were inevitable, with lines of division set along tribal boundaries.

Further tension has resulted from widespread reports that key sections of the animist community are on the verge of abandoning their traditional religions in favour of either Islam or Christianity. The tension has frequently given way to conflict and reports indicate that since 2000, an estimated 50,000 people have died in religious-motivated violence.[75] Throughout, Christian leaders have spoken out against violence and appealed for forgiveness on the basis of a just peace. Their voice would be sorely needed in February 2006 when the Prophet Mohammed cartoon controversy sparked Muslim attacks on Christian communities up and down the country. In the disturbances, 300 Christians died, prompting revenge attacks in which scores of Muslims were killed. The complete breakdown of relations between the two sides bodes ill for the future and efforts by the Christian community to find dialogue and co-operation are bound to be dogged by problems resulting from the growth of Islamist influence from known fundamentalist groups in Sudan, Saudi Arabia and other countries.

January 2005: Christian leaders in northern Nigeria challenged government statistics about the number of Christians killed by Muslim militants in clashes over the previous 12 months. The report produced by the government in Kano state claimed there were 84 Christian victims in 2004, but Church leaders put the figure at more than 3,000. Similarly, the Kano government claimed the Islamic extremists destroyed churches and private property amounting to US$70 million whereas the Christian Association of Nigeria valued the total as US$1.5 billion. Also in the state of Kano, government intelligence sources revealed that Islamic militants had secret plans for more attacks on Christians and their churches. The attacks were apparently aimed at destabilising the government and forcing the population to observe *Shari'a* law.

January 2005: Wearing the veil was made compulsory for girls in private schools in Kano State in the far north of Nigeria. The regulation even applies to non-Muslims. About 23 Christian girls were prosecuted for flouting the rule. The sale of alcohol was forbidden with a punishment of scourging for Muslims. Non-Muslims also have to abide by the new rule and if they break it they face a one-year prison term.

January 2005: In Bauchi State, central Nigeria, eight young women were given ten strokes of the lash for remaining unmarried.

February 2005: At least 36 people were killed and about 3,000 were forced to flee as violence swept through Demsa village, in the state of Adamawa, north-east Nigeria. The Christians who survived took refuge in the village of Mayolope in the nearby state of Taraba. On a visit to the refugees, the Governor of the state of Taraba, the Rev Jolly Nyame, called on the Nigerian government to control the activities of Islamic militants.

June 2005: A Christian professor, the dean of the faculty of law in the town of Zaria in the north of the country, disappeared after receiving a death sentence from a group of militant Muslims. It followed an accusation from hard-line Muslims in the university that he had blasphemed against the name of the Prophet Mohammed.

July 2005: In Kano, *Shari'a* was extended to cover all the inhabitants of the state, regardless of their religion. In the first law of its kind ever to come into effect in Nigeria, people were forbidden from travelling on any means of transport with members of the opposite sex. The 9,000 officers of the state religious police were instructed to enforce the new law, forbidding men and women from sitting together on buses.

August 2005: Fr Godwin Okwesili, a parish priest, was murdered in Lagos. It is alleged he was murdered by robbers bent on accessing his safe. The police were called to the scene, and later promised an investigation.

October 2005: Archbishop John Onayiekan of Abuja stated in an interview that Nigeria's Christian community may have been put at greater risk by the country's President, Olusegun Obasanjo, despite the fact that the politician is a Christian. He said: "It was naïve to think that his election could bring a better era for the Christians." The archbishop said the strongly anti-Muslim statements by Obasanjo may even have "created the conditions for still greater suffering by the Christians of the country". Archbishop Onayiekan went on to spell out the damage done to inter-faith relations by some evangelical Christian groups. He said: "[Theirs] is a religious outlook that has no regard for inter-religious dialogue; indeed it does not miss opportunities to speak ill of Islam and provoke tensions." He continued: "And when the conflict arrives, we are in the middle. The major clashes that have occurred in Nigeria have been provoked by these groups whereas the Catholic Church is the principal proponent of inter-religious dialogue."

February 2006: The appearance of cartoons of the Prophet Mohammed in the media in the West sparked perhaps one of the worst spates of inter-religious attacks in the modern history of Nigeria. In all, 300 Christians died in northern Nigeria and at least 100 Muslims. Fifty-eight people were killed and almost 50 churches were attacked when violence swept Borno State, centring on the capital, Maiduguri. Hundreds of shops and businesses were also targeted. Several of the faithful were murdered while they were praying and other Christians were lynched in the street. Among those who died was a Catholic priest, Fr Michael Gajere.[76] According to one report: "This priest was brutally murdered by a group of armed men, but not before having heroically brought to safety the altar servers present in the parish."[77] The priest's death prompted revenge attacks by Christians on Muslim communities in the southern Nigerian state of Onitsha, a Christian majority state in the south – up to 100 Muslims were killed. At least two mosques were burned. Elsewhere in the states of Borno and Katsina reports came in that 28 had died and over 200 were injured. Meanwhile, reports came in of tension soaring in the northern city of Bauchi, after rumours spread that the

Qur'an had been profaned by a school teacher, who had allegedly confiscated the text from a pupil caught reading it in class.[78] In the northern city of Kontagora Muslims armed with machetes killed nine Christians and set fire to four churches, while in Enugu in the south-east of the country, a group of Christian youths, armed with machetes and staves, beat to death a Muslim taxi driver and set fire to a mosque. A Christian girl, aged eight, had also been killed by a stray projectile. After the attacks, Fr George Ehusani, secretary general of the Nigerian Catholic bishops' conference, wrote in a communiqué that "the Episcopal Conference of Nigeria views with deep concern the unjustified mass killing of Christians… As always in these cases, these deplorable acts of ferocity in Maiduguri, just like the murders and reprisals in Onitsha and in other parts of the country, have been attributed to delinquents and faceless extremists. But this does not make these tragic events any less deplorable. We have reason to believe that the great majority of Muslims in this country are our neighbours, who love peace and respect the law. We call upon them, and in particular upon their leaders, to unite with us to isolate and eliminate from our society all those who promote and perpetrate violence and atrocities in the name of religion, which we hold dear."

March 2006: More than 460 people were arrested following violent clashes during the preceding two weeks between Christians and Muslims. According to the Inspector General of the police, Sunday Shindero, all those suspected of crimes were shortly due to appear in court and face trial.

North Korea

Population	Religions	Christian Pop.
30 million	Agnostic/Atheist 71.2%, New religions 12.9%, Animists 12.3%, Christians 2.1%, Others1.5%	600,000

One of the world's last communist countries, North Korea is as intolerant towards dissenters as it is militaristic in outlook. The late President Kim Il-sung is revered almost as a demi-god. His son and successor as head of state Kim Jong-il has continued to persecute followers of religions, especially Christians and Buddhists. The government says that religious liberty is respected and guaranteed by the constitution. But the reality is very different. The faithful are required to register in organisations controlled by the Party; those who are not enrolled, or who practise missionary activity, are subjected to violent persecution. Since the communist regime was established in 1953, about 300,000 Christians have disappeared and there are apparently no priests or religious left, most of them presumably murdered. Estimates put the number in prison camps at 80,000. According to ex-North Korean officials and prisoners, Christians in re-education camps and jails are treated much worse than other prisoners.

In the capital, Pyongyang, there are two Protestant churches and a Catholic one. Pro-regime propaganda is reportedly rife in the Protestant churches. For some ministers, the "beloved leader" Kim Jong-il is a demigod. Pyongyang boasts North Korea's one and only registered Catholic church.

North Korea's attitude to the Russian Orthodox Church has apparently been revolutionised with professed regime support for a new Orthodox church in Pyongyang. The favouritism is apparently aimed at boosting Russian aid for North Korea, whose economy is allegedly close to meltdown.

There are a great many people who try to leave the country, either for reasons of hunger or for religious reasons. If caught, they are either killed or required to do to forced labour. Those escaping to China can expect a raw deal. The Chinese leaders consider people fleeing North Korea to be "clandestine refugees" and forcibly repatriate them.

In 2005 the Catholic Church in South Korea undertook initiatives aimed at helping Christians in the North but progress is painfully slow.

February 2005: A 28-year-old North Korean refugee gave evidence at an international conference on human rights violations in North Korea. The woman, who cannot be named for safety reasons, reportedly said that forced infanticide and abortion remained common practice in the country's detention camps. She said this "is carried out with greater brutality against religious adherents".[79] She continued: "On one occasion, I glimpsed through a partly drawn curtain and with my own eyes I saw a nurse covering the face of a newborn child with a wet towel and suffocating it. The child stopped crying after about ten minutes." She added: "In the camps women are injected with substances to induce early labour". She herself had been captured in China, after having tried to flee there in 2000. After her arrest she was sentenced to two months in a detention camp in the province of Shinuiju, North Korea, and it was here that she witnessed the infanticide. In 2002 she succeeded in escaping to South Korea.

April 2005: The regime permitted "official" North Korean Catholics to mourn the death of Pope John Paul II.[80] Samuel Jang Jae-on, head of the Central committee of the Association of Korean Catholics, sent a message of condolence to the Holy See: "I express profound condolences. All the Catholics of our country are celebrating services in memory of John Paul II with profound sympathy both in the cathedral of Jangchung in Pyongyang and in the family places of worship in the country."

April 2005: About 100 people attended a Mass for Pope John Paul II at Pyongyang's Catholic church. The service was broadcast by a South Korean TV channel after permission was granted by the North. "When I heard the news of the death of the Pope," stated Kim Yong-ill, a priest of the Chang Chung Church in Pyongyang, "I was extremely surprised, for we did not even know he was ill."

May 2005: The diocese of Seoul approved the construction of a Korean National Centre for Reconciliation at Paju in Kyonggi province, close to the North Korean border. The diocese approved this project to "promote relations with the Church in North Korea and encourage a friendly approach" towards the inhabitants of the North. The building will have two storeys, one for use as a seminary and the other a place of prayer.

August 2005: The Rason International Catholic Hospital was opened in North Korea.[81] This hospital, in the province of Hamgyeongbuk-bo, was established by the Benedictine congregation of Saint Ottilien and by the

Catholic Church. With 100 beds in a building comprising three floors, the hospital will be staffed by a team of 80. Abbot Notker Wolf of the congregation of Saint Ottilien stated: "Catholic hospitals offer the hope of peace. I hope that this hospital in particular may open up another road towards cooperation."

August 2005: At a Mass marking the 160th anniversary of St Andrew Kim Dae-gon, the first priest and martyr of Korea, Cardinal Nicholas Cheong Jin-suk, the Archbishop of Seoul in South Korea, called on a crowd of 20,000 to "pray fervently" for the Church's mission in the North. Referring to the period before partition, he said: "There were 52 parishes and 50,000 Catholic faithful in the North, while there were around 100,000 in the South. After 1949 ... not a single priest was left alive in the North."

December 2005: Four North Korean Orthodox representatives travelled to the Russian city of Vladivostok for a course on ministry. The group, who were to live in St Nicholas's Cathedral, included a priest, two deacons and a student of sacred music. It was led by Peter Kim Chkher, president of the North Korean Orthodox committee. This committee was established in 2002 by the government and Fr Dionisy Pozdnyayev, a Russian Orthodox priest, at the invitation of the North Korean authorities.

December 2005: Russian Orthodox Archbishop Benjamin of Vladivostok and Primorye met a delegation led by Peter Kim Chkher, president of the North Korean Orthodox committee. The Korean delegation invited the archbishop to attend the consecration of the new Church of the Trinity, Pyongyang. The building was due to be completed in August 2006. When the site of the cathedral was blessed in June 2003, the North Korean government representatives apparently stressed the importance of Orthodox in Pyongyang practising their faith. They said they "hope" the Church would help strengthen ties between Russia and North Korea.

Pakistan

Population	Religions	Christian Population
160 million	Islam 95% Hinduism 1.7% Christianity 1.3% Others 2%	2 million

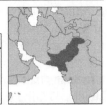

In the 18 months up to the end of June 2006, Christians and other minorities in Pakistan suffered the worst spate of persecution in Pakistan's 60-year history. A country carved out of British India in 1947 and intended as a 'home for Muslims' has quickly seen religion evolve from being a private, personal matter to becoming the defining characteristic of the nation-state, one which binds the people together on all levels – social, political and cultural. That this should have taken place so quickly is a reflection of the growth of fundamentalist Islam in a country with an estimated 40,000 *madrassas* (Islamic schools). The focus of aggression is not just centred on the Christian community. The persecution of followers of the Ahmadi religion is ferocious because although they follow many tenets of Islam, they do not recognise Mohammed as the last Prophet. In 2005 alone 11 Ahmadi were killed and 60 were subject to legal trials and punishment for religious reasons.

Increasingly, however, the radical Muslims' fury is centring on the Christians, whose co-religionists in the West are blamed for the world's ills. Christians are under threat from the Blasphemy Laws in which offences against the *Qur'an* are punishable with life imprisonment, and the death penalty can be invoked for insulting the Prophet Mohammed. But the attacks on Christian communities in Sangla Hill, east Pakistan, in November 2005, sparked by a Blasphemy Law allegation, showed that extremist Muslims are determined to 'avenge' Christians and others seen to be in cahoots with the West. Even then, few could have guessed the scale of the crisis in February and March 2006 when Pakistan's Christians were under attack from extremists outraged by media cartoons of the Prophet Mohammed. The damage – both physical and psychological – would seem to have brought Christianity in Pakistan to a new low from which it will be very hard to recover. The help of organisations such as *Aid to the Church in Need* is perceived by bishops and other clergy across the country to be vital as the country's Christian community goes through its darkest hour.

February 2005: About 20 people attacked the Catholic church in Kawanlit in Sialkot district. They broke the legs of a woman aged 70 and gravely injured another 50 people. The aggressors smashed the church's windows, desecrated the main altar and some sacred books. The group told the Christians that if they reported the incident, they would suffer further attacks. Behind the attack was a dispute over a plot of land, which the Church claimed was theirs but which was allegedly seized by a local Muslim, Mohammed Iqbal.

February 2005: Bashir Masih, a Christian aged 30, was condemned to seven years in prison for damaging a copy of the *Qur'an*. The judge said Masih had torn some pages out of the sacred book of Islam for use in an occult ceremony. The sentence was handed down by the civil court in a town in the diocese of Multan, on 23 February. News on the case then appeared to go silent, and Masih's whereabouts were unknown. Police said he owned up to the crime but reports later suggested it was a forced confession.

February 2005: Shahbaz Masih, a Christian trader in Punjab, was violently attacked with a knife by Ahmed Ali, one of his Muslim customers. After recovering in hospital, he returned home but was forced to close his shop and he and his mother left the village. Bishop Joseph Coutts of Faisalabad and a lawyer called Khalil Tahrir started legal proceedings against his attacker. Ahmed was briefly imprisoned but then released by the authorities under pressure from the extremists.

April 2005: A Muslim man called Ashiq Nabi was killed when 400 people went on the rampage in Spin Khak village, in the district of Nowshera in the North-West Frontier Province. During a family argument, on 18 April, Ashiq threw the *Qur'an* on the ground after his wife tried to make him swear upon it. Ashiq fled the house and later that day one of his uncles denounced him for blasphemy and the police began a search for him. Meantime, a local Muslim cleric issued an edict declaring Ashiq an "infidel" and worthy of death. Two days later he was discovered by the crowds who attacked him and he was shot dead. Police claimed they were searching for the cleric who issued the decree and wanted to arrest him but to no avail. The family of Ashiq refused to accept his body because he had been declared an infidel.

July 2005: A Christian baby died in the Kashmir town of Abottabad and the family was forced to travel south to bury her because the Islamic leadership in their home region refused to allow them to do so locally. En route, the family's lorry careered off the road following a landslide. Six of the relatives died in the accident and two others were injured.[82]

September 2005: Younis Masih, a 40-year-old Christian, was arrested by police. He was accused of using disrespectful language towards the Prophet Mohammed, while singing the *qwali* (a form of musical style in which verses on the prophets and saints of Islam are repeated). Following the incident, in Lahore, Younis was beaten by a crowd of local Christians, who were allegedly apologising. Then a group of Muslims beat him. During the night of 10 September around 200 men armed with sticks surrounded the local police station, demanding a blasphemy charge be brought against Younis. The crowd refused to leave unless their wishes were granted. Meantime, a group of Muslims attacked Younis' house and beat his wife. The next day 50 Christian families left the area for fear of reprisals and attacks by extremists. According to the police, Younis's life was in danger even though he was inside the police station. Following his confession, he was transferred to the prison of Kot Lakhpat.

12 November 2005: About 3,000 people torched three churches, a convent of religious sisters, two Catholic schools, the homes of two priests, a hostel for girls and the homes of many Christians in the town of Sangla Hill in the Punjab province. Fearing further violence, at least 450 Christian families fled from the town and did not return for more than two weeks. The violence was sparked by another case of alleged blasphemy. Yusif Said was accused of burning copies of the *Qur'an* before fleeing the scene of the crime. **(For the full story, see Interview with Yusif Said, page 66).** The Sangla Hill incident prompted Pakistan's Christian leaders to send a joint letter to Pakistan President Parvez Musharraf, calling for the immediate abolition of the blasphemy law. Referring to Sangla Hill, the Christian leaders have repeatedly stated: "The true assailants, namely those who are fomenting hatred, have not even been laid a finger on by the authorities. This state of affairs will lead to the destruction of harmony in the country and will risk becoming the cause of massive emigration."

November 2005: Archbishop Lawrence Saldanha of Lahore, the National President of the Justice and Peace Commission, stated at a press conference: "The attacks [against the Christian community of Sangla Hill]

63

were planned and organised." It followed eye-witness accounts which reported that the attackers were taken by bus into Sangla Hill from neighbouring towns and villages and were told to commit acts of violence and arson. He added: "Our people are living in fear and we want the government to do something." The council leader of Sangla Hill, Saqib Sohail Bhatti, also a Christian, told *Asia News* that the accusations of blasphemy were false.[83] The Justice and Peace Commission issued a statement: "The local police seem to be part of the cause of these acts of terrorism, which were using religion to disseminate hatred against the religious minorities." The commission calls for "an immediate judicial inquiry to establish the causes, effects and responsibility for these shameful incidents".

February/March 2006: Media cartoons of the Prophet Mohammed sparked Islamist aggression against Christians across Pakistan. On 14 February, about 100,000 people protested in Lahore, and threatened to storm the Sacred Heart Cathedral, Lahore. Terrified parishioners gathered in the cathedral and went ahead with Mass. Parish priest Fr Andrew Nisari said: "We thought we were in the middle of persecution – just like it was in the early Church. Under that kind of danger, we got so much courage... I said that even if they come while we are celebrating the Mass, I would not be afraid. I said there was no better way to die than at Mass."[84] On 19 February, 2,000 enraged Muslims rampaged through Sukkur, a town in Sindh province, attacking St Saviour's (Protestant) Church, and St Mary's (Catholic) Church.[85] Chalices, vestments and other sacred items were looted and burned but when the fundamentalist Muslims tried to break open the tabernacle door the handle snapped off. Visiting Sukkur shortly after, ACN projects staff discussed a request from Bishop Max Rodrigues of Hyderabad to help rebuild and enlarge the church. Immediately after the attacks, Sunday congregations at St Mary's doubled to 1,000. At an emergency meeting with clergy including Archbishop Lawrence Saldanha of Lahore, Pakistan Prime Minister Shaukat Aziz called on the bishops to report to the police any mosques inciting religious hatred.[86]

February 2006: A Presentation Sister in Peshawar feared for her life as she sheltered in an upstairs room as Muslim radicals broke into the premises including a school run by the convent.

June 2006: Christian convert, political activist and comparative religion scholar Yasaar Hameed, 36, appealed for asylum in Holland after facing police torture and attacks by Muslim extremists for his controversial religious views.[87] He applied for asylum in late March, meeting Dutch immigration officials for his first hearing on 7 June. Hameed has faced blasphemy charges since 1993.

June 2006: Speaking at an ACN conference in Portugal, Bishop Joseph Coutts of Faisalabad stressed concerns over the case of Javed Anjum, 19. The young man, who was confirmed in a ceremony led by Bishop Coutts, was lured to an Islamic school in Toba, 50 miles from Faisalabad, where it is alleged he was severely beaten after refusing to convert to Islam. Javed was subsequently taken to a police station where he dramatically revealed the identity of his attackers, before dying. Despite the fact that Javed's testimony was given on camera, the man allegedly held chiefly responsible for his death – the rector of the Islamic school – had yet to be brought to justice. Amid threats to the lawyer fighting on behalf of Mr Anjum's family, Bishop Coutts said: "We must keep up the pressure for justice. These Islamic groups are very powerful. They can make it look like an accident. They must admit that they have committed murder – it is against their religion."[88]

Interview with Yusif Said, a Christian from Pakistan

ACN UK, Interview in Pakistan
March 2006

IN NOVEMBER 2005, 46-year-old former buffalo trader Yusif Said had to run for his life after a dispute over a game of cards turned into a catastrophe, which shocked the world. Furious at losing to Yusif in the game of cards, his opponent accused him of burning pages of the *Qur'an* – a crime theoretically punishable by life imprisonment under Pakistan's Blasphemy Laws. The opponent, a Muslim, then demanded that local imams call for revenge not just against Yusif but against the whole Christian community where Yusif lived in the Punjab province. They ordered the Muslim faithful to assemble in front of the *Jamia Madni Masjid*, the central mosque, and urged them to act against the Christians who were "guilty of sheltering the fugitive blasphemer". Obedient to the last, the crowd began by ransacking the homes of both Yusif Said and his brother. They then torched the Presbyterian church, and the nearby pastor's house. Next they burned the Catholic church, the nearby convent of the sisters, and the house of the parish priest, Fr Samson Dilawar. Many miles away by this time, Yusif had run for his life and now he was totally helpless. But for him the torment had only just begun.

Yusif Said

One day I had an argument with a man over a game of cards. He demanded money from me and I refused to pay. Later the man came up to me and accused me of burning pages containing the *Qur'an*. I denied it and then he started shouting at me and people began gathering round and demanded that I own up to the crime. I refused and went away. I stayed the night with a Muslim friend of mine and when the police came, he told them I was innocent. Then I got a call from my cousin and it broke my heart to hear what he said.

The Muslim leaders had called for revenge for what I had allegedly done and 3,000 people rampaged through the Christian quarter of my home town of Sangla Hill, burning two churches and their adjoining schools, hostels and a convent. People's houses were ransacked. Two people were killed.

Fearing for the safety of my wife and children I gave myself in to the police. I said that I should meet face to face my accuser and that if he could prove my guilt I should be hung from a tree. I said: "Jesus will save me".

But instead of doing that, the police tied a rope through my legs and hung me from the ceiling. I was handcuffed. They told me to admit my guilt or reveal the culprit. They beat me with a slipper the length of my arm. For 14 days they kept me in police stations, moving from one to another no less than four times.

Eventually they charged me with desecrating the *Qur'an*, even though I had done no such thing. The courts gave me a guilty verdict. I told the judge I would not change the testimony I had originally given. They put me in jail and morning and evening I prayed to God and I believed that he would save me.

15 Muslims in jail became friendly and gave me some better food to eat. They knew that the man who accused me was a robber and that the case was bogus. Lawyers from the Church used what the Muslims were saying to challenge the court's decision. And then after three months and 22 days the ruling was overturned.

Looking back on my experience, I remember all the pain I endured, the beating, the pneumonia I suffered. All the time I prayed and I prayed with faith. I said that because of my faith I am saved. I kept thinking that if Christ has suffered why can't we?

But even though the courts changed their decision, I am not free. I have to stay in this safe house. There are 55 men in prison, guilty of the attack on the Christian quarter of Sangla Hill. Their families and friends would kill me if they got the chance.

I know that a lot of my problems would disappear immediately if I changed my faith. But I would rather be beaten and put to death than change my faith. It is Christ's love that has saved me.

Russia

Population	Religions	Christian Population
141.5 million	Christians 57.4% Agnostics 32.7% Muslims 7.6% Others 2.3%	81.2 million

The frosty approach of the dominant Russian Orthodox Church to the Catholic Church could yet thaw as circumstances of change and opportunity show signs of bringing the two closer together to confront common concerns. The gradual rehabilitation of the once all-powerful Russian Orthodox Church in the immediate post-Soviet era gave its leaders, especially Patriarch Alexy II of Moscow, increasing influence as it grew suspicious of the Catholic Church and other Christians, which were accused of proselytism. A stance of resistance reached its peak with Russian Orthodox dismay at the 2002 creation of four Catholic dioceses in Russia. Efforts by Pope John Paul II to build bridges with the Orthodox, especially with the return of the much-revered Icon of Kazan to Moscow, met with a response which many disappointed observers saw as muted.

But the election of Pope Benedict XVI in April 2005 has prompted Vatican and other commentators to signal that a slight – yet no less significant – shift in Russian Orthodox relations is apparent. Reports suggest the Orthodox hierarchy hold Pope Benedict's theological brilliance in deep regard. The new Pope's respect for tradition, both in liturgy and world affairs, is clearly not lost on Patriarch Alexy, especially in the search for a united front to challenge forces of materialism and secularism, which appear to have penetrated deep into Russian society, especially in the cities. Some observers hoped the registration of the Catholic diocese of Novosibirsk would bring an end to the long-running controversy over the development of Catholicism in the country. The last of four Catholic dioceses to receive official approval, many hoped that after the events in Novosibirsk, the issue would subside in Russian Orthodox minds. And yet the old charges of proselytism refuse to go away, as Patriarch Alexy continues to speak out against Catholic Church activities in neighbouring countries such as Kazakhstan and Ukraine, which the Moscow Patriarchate considers to be within the Russian Orthodox fold. And then there is the uncertain impact of the improving relations between the Catholic Church and the Greek Orthodox Church and its Istanbul-based Ecumenical

Patriarch, Bartholomew I, which looked set to take a higher profile especially with the Pope's visit to Turkey in late 2006. More delicate diplomacy will be the very least that is required if the Church's two ancient traditions – Orthodox and Catholic – are to grow in mutual respect and dialogue.

April 2005: Reports suggested the public were deeply moved by the death of Pope John Paul II and the election of Pope Benedict XVI but some nationalist parliamentarians said the widespread media coverage was part of "a propaganda campaign on behalf of the Vatican". Senior political commentator Leonid Radzichovskij said up to 25 percent of the electorate "inwardly agreed" with protestors' claims that "the Pope [John Paul II] is not a saint at all, but an anti-communist politician, linked to the CIA, whose principal achievement was to have caused the socialist system to crumble." It is not thought that these views were widely shared, as witnessed by the attendance of Metropolitan Kirill at John Paul II's funeral.

June 2005: A Russian Orthodox document was released criticising Protestants for "making a pact with humanism". The text, produced in April, criticises many Protestants for having secular tendencies adding: "A significant part of the Protestant world has made a pact with liberal humanism, further and further reducing its links with the Tradition of the Holy Church and changing the laws established by morality and dogmatic teaching." The document goes on to say the deviations had "led the Orthodox Church to rethink her relations with various confessions". It came in the same month as Patriarch Alexy called on Orthodox and Catholics to join together in tackling "the negative anti-Christian tendencies" in Europe.

July 2005: To mark the 1,000[th] anniversary of the foundation of the Shrine of Kazan, Patriarch Alexy II reinstated the Icon of the Mother of God, presented to him by Pope John Paul II in August 2004. The Patriarch stressed that a visit by the Pope to Russia was only possible if "there is a cessation of acts of proselytism by the Catholic Church in the territories of Russia, Ukraine and Kazakhstan".

November 2005: Newspapers published reports by Russia's justice ministry setting out plans to increase controls over foreign religious organisations including further restrictions on visas for foreign missionaries.[89] The plans

69

came in response to reports of highly pro-active evangelising religious sects. If implemented, the initiatives were seen as making it easier to suppress religious centres and increasing the red tape required for the registration of foreign bodies. The ministry's plans were reportedly in response to the expansion of foreign religions in Russia, which attracted government concern after news that the number of religious denominations in the country had increased from 29 to 69 within just ten years. Another aim of the plans was to step up efforts to stop illegal missionary work. The newspaper reports were not confirmed.

February 2006: Cardinal Roger Etchegaray visited Moscow at the invitation of Patriarch Alexy II. It followed a particularly active period of dialogue between the two Churches. One fruit of the flurry of diplomatic exchanges was the October 2005 decision to resume the joint Catholic–Orthodox commission. The commission was seen not only as a forum for dialogue to discuss the problem issues in the relationship but also as a means of setting out a framework for greater collaboration. Another fruit was the joint Catholic–Orthodox presentation of the Russian edition of the Compendium of the Social Doctrine of the Church. The event took place in Moscow in November 2005 and present was Cardinal Renato Martino, president of the Pontifical Justice and Peace Commission. The cardinal met Russian Orthodox Metropolitan Kirill and hopes were expressed about developing inter-Church dialogue not only at the hierarchical level but also involving dioceses and parishes.

July 2006: Leaders of different religions including Christianity, Islam, Judaism, Buddhism and Hinduism met in Moscow on the eve of the G8 Summit.[90] They discussed the importance of inter-faith dialogue as well as cultural and political exchange. The post-meeting communiqué read: "Dialogue and partnership among civilizations should not just be slogans." Religious freedom appeared later in the document: "We state the importance of religious freedom in today's world. Individuals and groups must be immune from coercion. No one is to be forced to act in a manner contrary to his or her own beliefs in religious matters. It is also necessary to take into account the rights of religious and ethnic minorities."

Saudi Arabia

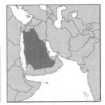

Population	Religions	Christian Population
27 million	Muslim 95.2% Christians 2.8% Others 2%	750,000

Culturally cut off from the West, Saudi Arabia is ruled over by the Al Saud family, whose strict enforcement of *Wahhabi Sunni* Islam means that political, social and especially religious freedom is forbidden. In the country of the Prophet Mohammed and the home of Islam's holiest sites – Mecca and Medina – non-Muslims have very little social status. Supported by a network of informants, the religious police arrest, imprison and torture people caught practising a faith other than Islam. There are crackdowns on people at worship in the privacy of their own homes. Saudi Arabia finances the construction of numerous mosques all over the world, but will not permit any churches or chapels to be built on its own soil. Non-Muslims – and even moderate Muslims – are persecuted by the religious police. A chemistry teacher received a 14-month prison sentence and 750 lashes to the hands for "deriding Islam". The man, who was Muslim, had allegedly discussed the Bible in class and spoken well of the Jews.

Among the Christian population, there is a high proportion of expatriates but they too are under the surveillance of the religious police. Some sources describe three 'layers' of churches in Saudi Arabia – 'tolerated fellowships' in embassies, underground house groups meeting in private homes and secret believers who do not meet in larger groups.[91]

February 2005: The US Select Committee on Religious Liberty called on the US government to impose sanctions against the Saudi regime for its systematic violation of religious rights.

March 2005: A Christian of Indian origin was arrested when a Bible was found on his person.

April 2005: Forty Pakistani Christians including children were arrested for taking part in a religious service at a private house in Riyadh.[92] The Saudi press claimed the church was 'inside' a large abandoned house, where the Pakistanis met every weekend. Inside, the security forces found: "books of

Christian propaganda, crosses, and a paralysed woman for whom the others were praying for healing, begging the intervention of God". In a report in the *Al Jazeera* daily newspaper, journalist Saud al-Shaibani said a Pakistani Muslim in the area "admitted to being influenced by Christian thought". Weeks later, the Saudi authorities still had not released any details about the incident and had taken no action. Archbishop Saldanha of Lahore called on the Pakistan government to act fast to secure the detainees' release. The archbishop said the arrest was "a grave episode of religious discrimination and a violation of human rights".[93]

April 2005: Religious police carried out a raid, arresting five leaders of a Christian community made up of about 60 Ethiopians and Eritreans.[94] Bibles were confiscated. About a month later, the five were released. They told how during part of their captivity they were tied up.

May 2005: Eight Christians of Indian origin were arrested after allegations that they were meeting to pray and study the Bible. Within a month seven were released on bail on condition that no further prayer meetings take place.

September 2005: US Secretary of State Condoleezza Rice called on the Saudi government to improve rights for religious minorities and threatened economic sanctions if no progress was made. More than four months later, The Centre for Human Rights in Saudi Arabia reported: "The Saudi government has still neither proposed nor applied any provision [of religious freedom]."

October 2005: As Ramadan got underway, the authorities threatened to expel Christians caught failing to observe the fasting regulations.

November 2005: For the second year running, the US State Department accused the Saudi regime of suffocating religious minorities. The comments were contained in the 7th Annual Report on Religious Liberty in the World, presented to the US Congress.

May 2006: Fr George Joshua from Kerela, India, was imprisoned for four days before being deported after seven religious policemen broke into a private house. The priest, who had just celebrated Mass, was arrested.[95] Archbishop Joseph Powathil, of Changanassery (Kerela) spoke out against the arrest on a visit to ACN UK's offices in Sutton, Surrey.[96]

Sri Lanka

Population	Religions	Christian Population
19.4 million	Buddhists 68.4%, Hindus 11.3%, Christians 9.4%, Muslims 9%, Others 1.9%	1.8 million

In other circumstances, the tsunami that decimated Sri Lanka's coastline and left 30,000 dead would have caused a divided country to pull together in a time of national emergency. But instead it brought to the surface issues which were unresolved despite the political agreement brokered after a 20-year civil war between the Tamil Tiger rebels in the north and the Colombo-based government. Religion was key to the conflict, a clash reinforced by cultural and ethnic differences, with the Hindu Tamil minority clashing with the Singhalese Buddhist majority. After the tsunami, an underlying religious motive was detected by Tamils and other minority religious groups outraged by the government's apparent failure to get aid through to the hardest-hit areas, where comparatively few Buddhists lived.

For Christians and other minorities, nothing could prepare them for a dramatic set-back for religious freedom, which followed the November 2005 Presidential elections. The new government of Mahinda Rajapakse announced plans to press ahead with proposed anti-conversion laws, deemed by Church leaders and others to be a threat to religious freedom.

The Act for the Protection of Religious Freedom set out to ban conversions and to stop anyone "seeking or assisting" to convert people. It carries a sentence of six years' imprisonment and a massive fine. Also proposed is an independent judicial system run by Buddhist monks, the Sanghadhikarana, or Buddhist court, which would judge cases brought by the inhabitants of the villages without reference to the police or the state courts.

The Bill on the Prohibition of Forcible Conversion requires every individual to inform the local authorities about his conversion within a specified period of time and that "no one shall convert or seek to convert persons from one religion to another by force or by fraudulent means". Sentences include a prison term of up to five years.

If the bills were passed by parliament in the form last seen in April 2006, observers believe they would create a climate of suspicion if not outright hostility for minority religious groups, most especially Christians.

March 2005: Catholic leaders in Sri Lanka accused the Colombo-based government of blocking aid relief to tsunami-affected areas.[97] Senior clerics in Sri Lanka claimed that politics and religion were getting in the way of emergency humanitarian work, which had only just begun despite the overwhelming international response to the disaster. The worst affected areas were places populated mostly by religious minority groups – Hindus, Christians and Muslims, who were dependent on the government in Colombo for the transfer of aid. Christian leaders reported that the government had refused access to aid consignments, delayed the transport of relief materials and stymied international aid operations. Leading the criticism of Sri Lanka's government, Fr Sunil De Silva, Secretary to Archbishop Oswald Gomis of Colombo, said: "I have been so moved by the amount of aid people have been sending us but the government are making life so difficult. They should have a little bit of concern for the people."

May 2005: The Bill on the Prohibition of Forcible Conversion was approved in part by Parliament. Amendments were made after the Supreme Court declared that two clauses contravened the country's constitution, which defends the individual's right to choose their religion. The bill was due to go to a standing committee before a final reading in Parliament. Catholic bishops said that "in characterising as proselytism the social work of the Church, such as orphanages or help for the poor, this proposed law will also hit the most defenceless members of the population."

May 2005: UN religious liberty special reporter Asma Jahangir arrived in Sri Lanka to meet with Buddhist, Hindu and Christian representatives. In a press conference in Colombo on 12 May, Jahangir said she had found no proof of forced conversions, which Buddhist leaders alleged were rising sharply. Some Buddhist monks described the "urgent" need for new laws to combat the problem. Jahangir said: "The two anti-conversion laws will end up by persecuting and not protecting the religious minorities and will hinder the promotion of coexistence between the various different communities."

May 2005: Bishop Joseph Vianney Fernando of Kandy reported that Pope Benedict XVI was "concerned" by the anti-conversion laws.[98] The bishop's comments came after the Sri Lankan bishops' *ad limina* meeting with the Pope. "Each one of us," he reported, "has spoken with the Pontiff about this terrible law and he has assured us of his prayers and invited us to continue our campaign in defence of religious liberty". During the run-up to the elections, senior figures in Sri Lanka, especially in the Church, appealed to the Presidential candidates to clarify their policies on the anti-conversion laws. Presidential candidate Mahinda Rajapakse (who later triumphed at the polls) accused Archbishop Oswald Gomis of Colombo of making a thinly-veiled attack against him during a speech. The archbishop defended his speech, saying: "I have heard speeches promoting anti-Christian laws" and encouraging hatred. Bishop Joseph Vianney Fernando, president of the Catholic bishops' conference of Sri Lanka, said supporters of the laws had been prompted by Christian evangelicals: "For 20 years now fundamentalist Christian groups have been waging an aggressive campaign of conversions, exploiting the conditions of poverty and the needs of the population. These actions greatly disturb the Buddhist majority and are a source of concern for the Church herself, in as much as Catholics are the most affected."

May 2005: In Batticaloa a Methodist church was burnt down. Eyewitnesses blamed Buddhist militants.

May 2005: The police of Milepost, in the district of Polonnaruwa, threatened to arrest the pastors of a local church, ordering them to stop their religious activities and to abandon plans to build more churches in the town, which was considered a 'Buddhist area'.

July 2005: The Holy Family Church in Kayankerny, Batticaloa city, east Sri Lanka, was badly damaged after explosions went off nearby. On the same day, 7 July, masked men set fire to a Catholic church in Pulasthigama, in Anuradhapura diocese, north-east of Colombo. The parish priest, Fr Eric Fernando, said the attackers wanted to cause maximum harm. Again in July another Catholic church was attacked in Patunagama.

July/August 2005: Intimidation and threats by a crowd of Buddhists forced leaders of a Christian church in Horana, in the Kalutara district, to close the building to worshippers on two successive Sundays.[99] Police ordered them to suspend worship because they were "disturbing the peace". The faithful were told not to hold religious activities elsewhere.

November 2005: Sri Lankan Prime Minister Mahinda Rajapakse, of the Sri Lankan Freedom Party (SLFP), emerged victorious in the Presidential elections, beating Ranil Wickremesinghe, by just 2 percent of the vote. The new president immediately nominated Ratnasiri Wickremanayake as his Prime Minister who, at the age of 73, was considered a veteran hawk regarding the Tamil Tigers, to whom he had consistently refused concessions. Wickremanayake, a former Minister for Buddhist affairs, was the main promoter of the Act for the Protection of Religious Freedom, the harsher of the two proposed anti-conversion laws. By contrast, no ministerial post was given to the Jathika Hela Urumaya (JHU), the allied nationalist party made up of Buddhist monks, which is responsible for the other piece of religious legislation under consideration, the Bill on the Prohibition of Forcible Conversion. The JHU however promised to support the new government.

December 2005: Joseph Parajasingham, a Catholic Tamil parliamentarian, was killed in Batticaloa's Catholic cathedral, during Christmas Midnight Mass on 24 December. Parajasingham was a member of the Tamil National Alliance, a formation supported by the Tamil Tigers. The motive remains unclear.

June 2006: Six people were killed and scores of others were injured when a church was attacked in a clash between the Sri Lankan Navy (SLN) and the Liberation Tigers of Tamil Eelam.[100] The incident took place in Pesalai, Mannar district, on the coast in northern Sri Lanka. Having shot five fishermen at point blank range, the SLN made for the Church of Our Lady of Victory, killing a 75-year-old woman and wounding many others. The victims were of different faiths. Urging forgiveness, Bishop Rayappu Joseph of Mannar blamed the SLN for the attack.

Sudan

Population	Religions	Christian Population
35 million	Muslims 70.3% Christians 16.7% Animists 11.9% Others 1.1%	5.8 million

The signing of the Comprehensive Peace Agreement (CPA) between the Khartoum-based government of Sudan and the Sudanese People's Liberation Army/Movement (SPLA/M) on 9 January 2005 was popularly hailed as a milestone in the country's hard-won search for peace.

The agreement promised to bring a formal end to one of the worst conflicts in modern African history between the Islamist-controlled Muslim north and the Christian/Animist south. In 25 years of unmitigated misery, 2.5 million people were killed and more than four million were rendered homeless, giving Sudan the dubious honour of having the world's largest population of internally displaced people.

Building on the CPA's gigantic step forward, the Parliament in Khartoum unanimously approved a new constitution. Acknowledging that Sudan has "considerable communities" of Christians, Article 1 states: "Sudan is a welcoming country where races and cultures merge and [where] religions are reconciled."

The constitution gave added emphasis to the CPA's stated aim of a six-year period of autonomy for south Sudan followed by a referendum with an option for independence.

For many the deal seemed almost too good to be true. Then, dramatically, SPLA/M leader Dr John Garang died in a helicopter crash just three weeks after taking office as Vice President, an appointment agreed as part of the peace treaty.

While ever hopeful of a long-term resolution to the country's tribal, religious and cultural disputes, Church leaders have expressed concerns about the ambitions of the Government of Sudan. It is thought to be undeniable that Khartoum is determined to enforce *Shari'a* beyond the confines of the north and that resources both financial and human are being expanded to consolidate Islam in the south.

Indeed, Sudan observers suggest that the government has only sued for peace in the south to concentrate its efforts in the Darfur region in the west, where Khartoum-backed *Janjaweed* Islamists have stoked a conflict that by mid-2006 had claimed an estimated 200,000 lives.

Hence, for Christians, especially those in and around Khartoum, the problem of oppression continues to cast a long shadow over their lives. From 1999, Church leaders noticed some change in the government attitude towards the Church – for example entry and stay permits for expatriate missionaries are more readily granted and the harassment of diocesan schools has practically disappeared. In fact, Church leaders report that in four cases plots were allotted for diocesan-run schools. That said, a relatively new and major problem is the expropriation of Church land and property under the pretext of 'land enhancement/upgrading', which corresponds to the policy applied in the 1990s of demolishing Church schools and prayer centres in the name of town planning. Access to essential services such as health care is still restricted for Christians and many of them are barred from jobs on account of their faith.

Indeed, while there are glimmers of hope, the Church still faces a struggle for its very existence. Just one example of the challenges still faced is that apostasy – the conversion of a Muslim to another religion – is still punishable by death, theoretically at least. For Sudan's Christians, there may at last be an end to war, but the search for a peace in which they are free to practise their religion, is still a long way off.

February 2005: The Catholic bishops of Sudan made a statement about the CPA. "True peace is much more than the absence of war. What is needed now are our prayers, together with the individual and collective efforts to ensure that the peace is an effective one. The peace that we are seeking to build is an order and a harmony within the community, such that individuals and communities can develop in fullness and freedom. This labour of building peace has social, economic, political, cultural and religious aspects."[101]

March 2005: Describing the humanitarian crisis in Darfur, Monsignor Fortunatus Nwachukwu, a councillor on the permanent Mission of the Holy See at the United Nations, spoke of a crisis which by then had caused two million to flee their homes: "The precarious condition of life in which millions of people are forced to live, torn away from their villages and their native lands, demands concrete and rapid decisions to alleviate their sufferings and protect their rights."[102] He denounced "systematic attacks on the civilian population and the destruction of infrastructure and of entire villages. The attacks are brutal and violent and the violation of human rights a daily occurrence."

April 2005: Monsignor Peter Ayuong, vicar general of the Catholic diocese of Khartoum, was arrested.[103] Auxiliary Bishop Daniel Adwok of Khartoum, who was with Monsignor Ayuong when the incident happened, recalled: "Two agents in civilian clothes came and knocked at the door of our house. After a brief discussion they arrested the priest, handcuffed him and took him to the police station in Khartoum, from   where he was then transferred to the prison of Wad Medani." The police accused Fr Ayuong of having paid for a car with an unsecured cheque. "It is nothing more than a pretext [for the arrest]," continued Bishop Adwok. He said the real reason for the arrest was the government's wish to seize land belonging to the diocese. Fr Ayuong was later released. The charges against him were dropped because none of the supposed witnesses to his crime appeared in court. However, on 23 May, Fr Ayuong was arrested again by men in civilian clothes who frogmarched him to the police station. Fr Ayuong was then transferred once again to Wad Medani, from where the arrest warrant had been issued. Only after several hours was he released by the authorities.

May 2005: The Khartoum daily newspaper *Al Wafaq* was suspended for several days and its editor, Mohammed Taha, was arrested after publishing an article deemed blasphemous against the Prophet Mohammed. The government controls imports of religious publications. Occasionally, newspapers are banned from printing, usually for political motives, but sometimes also for religious reasons.

August 2005: Cardinal Gabriel Zubeir Wako, Archbishop of Khartoum, appealed for calm after the capital erupted in violence after SPLA/M leader and newly installed vice president Dr John Garang died in a helicopter accident.[104] On 29 August, the cardinal said Garang's message of hope and peace would be continued by his successors. The cardinal stressed the importance of freedom of rights and fair distribution of resources.

September/October 2005: Cardinal Zubeir declared: "The masquerade of peace in Sudan produces poverty and injustice, which continue to threaten the population."[105] He also criticised Western governments, accusing them of failing to listen to the Church. Addressing 400 people at *Aid to the Church in Need*'s Westminster Event, in September 2005, the cardinal said: "If I tell you that the Christians are persecuted and that our life is difficult, how long will it take you to listen to me? How many realise that I put my life in danger by talking to you?"[106] The cardinal said that students were "brainwashed" in government schools, that the police and security forces had put the country "under lock and key" and that the Church did not have the right to own property. He emphasised that in the north of the country many non-Muslim citizens were under pressure to accept the *Shari'a*, and that the government were using public resources to "Islamise" the south, where peace was constantly under threat.

April 2006: In an interview, Bishop Cesare Mazzolani of Rumbek, south Sudan, said: "Islam is invading us, and if we do not do something very quickly the Islamists will defeat us with their superior power."[107] The bishop said Muslims were pursuing "the clear objective of dominating the whole country with the laws of Islam... They present themselves as benefactors, but in reality they are seeking to literally buy the conversion of the people. They think they are the masters." It is therefore necessary, concluded the bishop, "to act immediately, because otherwise there will not be time. We will never give in, but if we do not establish development and education, then the battle will be lost."

Interview with Bishop Daniel Adwok of Khartoum

ACN UK, published in *The Catholic Times*
June 2004

"IN THE NAME OF GOD, do you accept?" The two men stood face to face. It was now or never. Standing on the airfield with the engines of the plane beginning to whirr into action, the apostolic nuncio glanced at the aircraft and then back at the man who was proving so obstinate. But Daniel Adwok Marco Kur was not going to be rushed. He was used to turning people down when he had to.

His people, in the Sudanese town of Malakal, were desperate for help. Not long before, the military had descended on the place and literally flattened every building in sight, regardless of who might be inside. As the parish priest, Fr Adwok had opened up the parish centre compound to more than 2,500 people. It was to be their refuge for weeks on end. While most slept in the back yard, the veranda was made available to young mothers so they could look after their toddlers and babies under cover from the rains. In a sign of the people's trust, Fr Adwok was given responsibility for distributing the food supplies brought down the White Nile once a year.

And so when one day, Fr Adwok was told he had been named a bishop, his gut reaction was to refuse. Recalling the event, which took place in 1992, Bishop Adwok said: "I was told that the apostolic nuncio was coming to see me and the people sent me to go and find him. But I said he should come to me. I needed relief for the people. I wanted him to see what was going on here. We thought the young mothers and the children under the veranda were in risk of getting pneumonia and we wanted to find somewhere out of the rain for them to be warm and dry. I felt he should see that."

But the town authorities held sway and Fr Adwok duly left the parish to report to the nuncio. No doubt, the nuncio had expected the meeting to be a formality but as Fr Adwok began to resist his nomination as bishop, the discussion grew heated. With no conclusion in sight, the conversation continued as they walked back to the nuncio's plane.

Bishop Adwok recalled: "I kept telling him: 'The people need me' and I reeled off a list of other priests who could be the bishop. But eventually, when he explained that he was acting under the instructions of the Holy See and that they needed an answer immediately, I reluctantly said yes."

This blend of compassion and determination is a recurring theme in the life story of Bishop Adwok. The bishop, who is based in Kosti, south of Khartoum, explained how his life's work was about restoring dignity to the downtrodden Christian communities. "For me," he explained, "the biggest challenge has been the inability to build a true Christian community."

Week in, week out for months and years on end, Bishop Adwok's task has been to rally the faithful who have again and again become the innocent victims of the war between the Government of Sudan, the Islamic regime in the north, and the rebel army in the south.

Unable to protect themselves, the Christian communities were targeted by Islamic militia, who mistook them for supporters of the southern-based rebels, the SPLA/M. Undaunted, Bishop Adwok confronted the aggressors head-on. One recent example took place in a football stadium in central Khartoum. Crowds gathered after the disappearance of two priests. They were putting pressure on the bishops to reveal what they knew.

"We wanted to deal with these questions once and for all," said Bishop Adwok, "and so I went out there and told them that we thought the priests were being detained by security forces and that we were concerned for their safety. We thought it was possible they were being tortured. I told the people that the priests' innocence was beyond question." It was a risky move – one that put him at risk of reprisals from the government. But the gamble paid off and Bishop Adwok continued his ministry unmolested.

There has been plenty to do. Hundreds of thousands of Christians in the south fled north to escape the worst of the fighting and Bishop Adwok's diocese has been host to many of these homeless people, who have set up mud hut shanty towns that have considerably enlarged the city of Khartoum. Deprived of the most basic resources and living in the baking heat of the desert, these communities are easy targets for government initiatives to demolish their homes and disperse them even further into the desert – all in the name of so-called "city planning".

Now that peace has come between the government and the SPLA/M, Bishop Adwok is at the forefront of an initiative by the bishops to ensure that such abuses against the Christians are stopped. He has lobbied key figures in the international community to take action to crack down on the persecution.

The litany of complaints includes denial of visas for Christian visitors to Sudan and acute problems for Christians getting jobs. The list goes on but among the most serious is that Christian women have been whipped for breaking strict Islamic *Shari'a* law by failing to cover their heads.

"The fact of the matter is that Christians are treated as second class citizens," said Bishop Adwok. Physical abuse extends to children and young people. Bishop Adwok's security guard, James, 20, said that teachers at the government-run school he attends regularly beat him with a stick for insisting on missing a class to go to Sunday Mass. And yet he is undaunted: "I am a Christian. It is my duty to go to Church and nobody has the right to take that away from me."

Nor do the problems end there. In the region of Kosti, the area of Khartoum diocese for which Bishop Adwok is responsible, he said there was only one legally-recognised church.

Listening to such challenges facing the Church, I suppose it is no wonder that sadness, frustration and even anger well up inside. But aggression could not be further from the case where Bishop Adwok is concerned. And yet he has every excuse to be resentful. When he was barely a teenager, his father was killed when the first civil war broke out in Sudan in 1964. It meant he and his family had to work for a living whilst struggling on with their education.

Instead, it is reconciliation that Bishop Adwok preaches but on the basis of truth and justice. "I suppose what matters to me is service," he said. "I am moved to service of the people, whether it is material service or defence of their rights. Even if I am not strong enough to stand up for them, I feel I should be a friend, someone who'd like to share in their difficulties."

Turkey

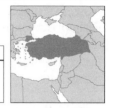

Population	Religions	Christian Population
73.3 million	Muslims 97.2% Atheists 2.2% Christians 0.6%	440,000

The secular constitution of modern Turkey holds out the promise of religious freedom to all. The media holds up Turkey as a prime example of a Muslim country with a welcoming attitude to minorities. Indeed, in 2005 Turkey's secular government re-asserted the country's tolerance-to-all credentials with a package of reforms including a prison term for religious rights offences.

Restraining Islamic practice remains part of government policy with a continued ban on Muslim women wearing the veil in public. Turkey's President Necdet Sezer recently blocked a ruling passed by Parliament to decriminalise preaching the *Qur'an* in places other than those authorised by the State.

The Church has fared badly with continued delays by the Turkish Parliament to pass a law recognizing the legal status of the Churches, a bill dating back years and one considered as a pre-condition of Turkey's entry into the European Union.

Away from the Turkish government, aggressive anti-Christian forces are at work. Christians are targeted in sporadic attacks, with one particularly bloody case in 2006. The fact that the overwhelming majority of the population are *Sunni* Muslims means that safeguards against intolerance are often found to be lacking. While long-standing antipathy towards Greece may explain the continued pressure on the Istanbul-based Greek Orthodox Patriarch, anti-Christian sentiment also explains why his residence has tight security following a string of attacks. The scheduled visit to Turkey of Pope Benedict XVI planned for autumn 2006, is certain to bring to the surface ongoing tensions between the State, Islam and the freedoms of minority groups.

March 2005: The Minister for Religious Affairs, Mehmet Aydin, told Parliament that the missionaries were threatening the unity of the nation.

He added: "The aim of their activities is to threaten the cultural, religious, national and historical unity of the Turkish people."[108] Such a 'threat' would seem miniscule on the basis of reports showing that in Turkey there were just 368 conversions to Christianity in the past five years. The minister urged support for initiatives to overcome the "missionary propaganda", which "has a historical background and is conducted in a planned manner with political motives." The Minister said the Ministry for Religious Affairs should "enlighten the Turkish people, eradicate the ignorance and defend the moral principles and beliefs of Islam". His remarks brought a sharp protest from the EU ambassador who described the minister's comments as "divisive".

April and June 2005: The US Ambassador to Turkey made two official protests about attacks on Protestant groups. Ten incidents of this kind have apparently taken place in as many months. None of these attacks were officially reported in the national press because the Christians are too afraid to come forward for fear of reprisals.

June 2005: Reports indicated government approval of plans to pass a plot of land once occupied by a church to Kurdish Muslims.[109] The Syrian Orthodox owned the site in the village of Bardakci, where the Church of Our Lady once stood. After gaining possession of the land, the Kurds look set to defy the protests of the Christian minority by building a mosque.

August 2005: Hundreds of Muslims went on the rampage in the Greek Orthodox quarter of the town of Altinozu. The Muslims, who had come from the town of Karsu, shouted: "There is no room for the infidels here." Five people were injured, including the wife of the priest, and ten houses were damaged during the attack. The clash was triggered by a dispute that same evening between young people of the two towns, clashes which led to the arrest of two Orthodox youths, accused of using a razor to attack two Muslims.

September 2005: The president of the Turkish republic, Ahmet Necdet Sezer, invited Pope Benedict XVI to visit Turkey in 2006, so that he "could witness for himself the climate of cultural tolerance" prevailing in the country. It followed an earlier invitation from the Greek Orthodox Patriarch Bartholomew I, following a now established tradition started by Pope Paul VI and continued by John Paul II.

January 2006: Protestant pastor Kamil Kiroglu, from a church in Adana, was beaten unconscious by five men who threatened to murder him if he did not convert to Islam. They gained entrance by pretending to be newly converted Christians from Turkmenistan, before kicking and punching him. They shouted: "We don't want Christians in this village." They put a knife to his throat and threatened him: "Renounce Jesus, or we will kill you". The minister Kiroglu responded by repeating: "Jesus is Lord".

February 2006: An Italian Catholic priest, Fr Andrea Santoro, was shot dead in the Church of Our Lady, Trebisonda. A Muslim youth was held responsible. The murder was followed by Turkish media reports accusing the priest of proselytism. But speaking to journalists, Monsignor Luigi Padovese, the Vicar Apostolic of Anatolia, said: "the true motive for the murder of Don Santoro was religious excitation, motivated by the anti-Christian climate" in the region, "in the families, the schools and the written literature". Asked about the situation of the Christians in Anatolia, Monsignor Padovese described it as "not easy". He continued: "The only news put about regarding the Catholic Church is either defamatory of Christianity or trivial." The Catholic cemetery in Trebisonda had been flattened by bulldozers, he said. The gravestones have been defaced "and now there are only three headstones left. Just a few days before his death, Don Andrea had contacted the local Mayor asking for a protective fence around what is now a wasteland." The comments coincided with a threat by a group of Muslims against the Slovenian Catholic priest in Smyrna. The Muslims shouted at Fr Martin Kmetec: "We will kill you all; Allah is great."

June 2006: A man, allegedly a schizophrenic, attacked Fr Pierre Brunissen, 75, in the northern city port of Samsun. The priest, who was attacked with a knife, was taken to hospital with injuries to his thigh. Bishop Luigi Padovese, Vicar Apostolic of Anatolia, told ACN of media hostility, including fabricated reports that Fr Pierre had tried to bribe people to win converts. The bishop spoke of a media-led campaign to undermine the success of Pope Benedict XVI's scheduled visit to Turkey in late November 2006. He said: "The newspapers are trying to aggravate, to show the Christians as enemies of Turkish people." He added that "many, many people" were opposed to the planned meeting between the Pope and Ecumenical Patriarch Bartholomew I of Istanbul.[110]

Vietnam

Population	Religions	Christian Population
84.4 million[111]	None 80.8% Buddhist 9.3% Christian 7.2% Others 2.7 %	6 million

When Communist North Vietnam seized control of the South in 1975, concern for the future of Christianity spread far and wide. But the oppression that undoubtedly followed began to ease from the early 1990s. It coincided with a surge in vocations. Fears of a new clamp down on the Church resurfaced with the 2004 "Ordinance on Religion and Religious Belief". Although a number of religious were released from prison in the wake of the ordinance, clergy spoke out saying the new ruling would signal a return to the repressive 1980s. Concerns were raised that the ordinance would tighten the controls on the Church with regulations on a wide range of religious activities from restrictions on travel for clergy to an upper limit on religious retreats. Some Vietnam observers suggest however that the sheer growth of the Church means the government will not try to enforce the ordinance to the letter. With over 3,000 religious sisters and 500 priests in South Vietnam's Ho Chi Minh diocese, religious and lay alike look set to assert their growing confidence, even in the face of continuing opposition. The Church's resilience has been further buoyed up by the ordination in November 2004 of 57 new priests in Hanoi Cathedral and the creation of the new diocese of Ba Ria the following month.

January 2005: The government marked the New Year by announcing that 8,325 prisoners would be released. Among those due to be freed were dissident politicians, Buddhists and Christians including Fr Nguyen Van Ly, aged 59. Fr Ly, imprisoned since 2001, was convicted of sabotage, endangering national security and other plots. He had been condemned to 15 years' imprisonment at the time. Reports suggested he was in fact condemned for sending a letter abroad in which he described attacks on religious liberty.[112] Vietnam observers say the release of the dissidents is a sign of "new change" by the Hanoi-based government.

January 2005: Redemptorist priest Fr Chân Tin, aged 83, released a document denouncing the government's "repressive policy towards religion".[113] The priest said the oppression came about as a result of a combination of laws, which by themselves did not necessarily represent a problem. One example he gave was of a law which stated that worship was only permissible in authorised buildings. Another law stated that before new religious buildings could be erected, state permission was required. Hence the government could refuse proposed church buildings and stop authorised worship. The document ends up by asking: "Is not the ultimate aim of the State to force all the religions to submit to its control?".

February 2005: A religious sister from Vietnam, who cannot be named for safety reasons, described 2004's "Ordinance on Religion and Religious Belief" as a "throw-back" to the 1980s – one of the darkest periods of state-sponsored intimidation against the Church.[114] According to the nun, newly-elected religious superiors would require government approval, the number of priestly ordinations would be limited, and clergy would require permission to travel, even within the country. But the sister said the Church would not buckle under oppression. "We want to obey the [new] laws but if the government interferes with our religious life, we have no option but to refuse to accept them… If the government asks us what we are doing, we will dialogue with them. But if they do not listen, we will carry on anyway." The sister said Christians were emboldened by the Church's growth. "It's amazing – the more difficult things get, the more the Church seems to grow. If you go into any Church at Easter and Christmas, you can see there are a lot of conversions – especially of young people."

May 2005: The USA "recognised the steps taken by the country in the field of religious liberty".[115] A few hours before the historic visit by the Vietnamese Prime Minister Phan Van Khai to Washington on 21 June, Robert Zoellick, the US Assistant Secretary of State, met with a delegation of representatives of the Vietnamese authorities, in particular the Vice Prime Minister Vu Khoan, and the minister for planning and investment, Vo Hong Phuc, with whom he signed an agreement "with regard to the respect for religious liberty".

July 2005: The Vatican expressed "the hope that it will be possible to advance rapidly" towards the "normalization" of relations with Vietnam. The communist authorities have had no formal diplomacy with the Holy See.

September 2005: The government permitted St Joseph's Major Seminary in Hanoi to admit new seminarians every year. St Joseph's, in common with seminaries in Ho Chi Minh City (Saigon) and Xuan Loc, had been permitted to accept new students every other year, and always only in limited numbers.[116]

May 2006: The Mennonite Church of Vietnam in Ho Chi Minh City was raided by about 50 public security officials in connection with a grievance against a building permit being used by the church.[117] During the attack on the church and office, the security officials reportedly beat church members and construction workers alike. Some church members were badly injured after being pushed from a height of five metres onto a concrete floor. A number of church members were arrested. According to *Compass Direct News*, on 8 May the Rev Quang, the church leader, had secured a permit to rebuild the church. During the raid, authorities claimed that the construction work exceeded the scope of the permit. The attack was symptomatic of the continued oppression suffered by lesser-known Churches.

Zimbabwe

Population	Religions	Christian Population
12.9 million	Christians 67.5%, Animists 30.1% Others 2.4%	8.7 million

With its economy in tatters and its people devastated by poverty and mass unemployment, few, if any, have escaped the crisis engulfing Zimbabwe. Repression and violence are commonplace in a country torn apart by conflict and the suffering has affected people whatever their religious beliefs.

The constitution guarantees religious liberty, but the government does not always respect this right. There is no state religion and all religions are recognised. Religious institutions do not have to register, unless they run schools or hospitals. Teaching of religion in private schools is permitted.

The success of President Robert Mugabe's ZANU-PF party in the elections of March 2005 put Zimbabwe under renewed pressure with claims of electoral fraud. At a time of severe food shortages, the government was embroiled in a 'food for votes' scandal. In a series of amendments to the constitution, the government awarded itself the right to confiscate land and to withdraw passports from people considered a threat to national security. The widespread demolition of shanty towns led to claims that almost three million urgently needed food aid.

Christian leaders, who have criticised the Mugabe regime, have been threatened, arrested and imprisoned. Among the most outspoken critics has been Archbishop Pius Ncube of Bulawayo. Relations between Church and State, which formerly had been fruitful, have come under intense strain as the bishops have sought to speak up for a people desperate for food, jobs and security. Despite the difficulties, the few reports that come through from the Church indicate that the Christian community is strong in faith and determined to help a people whose country is in crisis.

March 2005: In a pastoral letter, timed to coincide with the start of the Presidential elections, the Catholic bishops of Zimbabwe issued an appeal for peace and fair play. "We invite all Christians to pray for our leaders and candidates, that they adopt a policy that is respectful of human dignity. Let our leaders be people who are God-fearing, and capable of overcoming false attitudes, just as Jesus did when he was tempted in the desert."

August 2005: In a report to ACN, a priest from Harare described how people had begged him for food and shelter after their shack-like homes were destroyed under government orders.[118] The priest, who cannot be named for security reasons, told how he had taken the homeless people to so-called 'communal areas' and provided them with blankets and maze to eat. He said: "We are not really allowed to distribute food but people are so hungry and we feel we must do something." As well as distributing food parcels every day, the priest told how he was putting up 300 very basic homes made of plastic and wood. *Aid to the Church in Need* has given key help to support the priests so they can minister to the people in their hour of need. ACN has helped nearly 40 seminarians in Harare, who have no roof on the church.

December 2005: A priest from Zimbabwe described "the beautiful simplicity" of his Christmas festivities celebrated amid desperate poverty and huge uncertainty about the future.[119] In a rare message from a country increasingly cut off from the outside world, the priest from the capital, Harare, described how his Christmas Masses went ahead despite people suffering from a severe shortage of petrol and money. Telephone lines were down, there were constant power cuts and travel was hampered by heavy rains. The priest, who requested anonymity, described how power was restored briefly at about 10pm on Christmas Eve, just in time for midnight Mass. In the offertory, he received a chicken and a goat, which provided him with lunch on Christmas Day. In spite of all the problems, the priest's message was full of joy. He added: "Despite the power cuts and the constant rains, we had a lovely Christmas – Midnight Mass was beautiful in its simplicity."

[1] *Rapporto 2006 sulla Libertà Religiosa nel Mondo,* Aiuto alla Chiesa che Soffre, 2006

[2] *BBC News,* 31.3.06

[3] *BBC* Country Profiles (United Nations 2005). Most total population figures in this book are taken from this source.

[4] *United Nations*

[5] *Compass Direct News*

[6] *Rapporto 2006*

[7] *ACN UK News,* 24.8.05

[8] *UCAN News Service*

[9] *World Christian Encyclopaedia,* 2001

[10] *Rapporto 2006*

[11] *Rapporto 2006*

[12] *Christian Solidarity Worldwide*

[13] *BBC News*

[14] *ACN UK News,* 23.2.05

[15] *Rapporto 2006*

[16] *ACN UK News,* 24.11.05

[17] *Forum 18*

[18] *World Evangelical Alliance, Religious Liberty Committee*

[19] *Christian Freedom International*

[20] *ACN UK News*

[21] *Christian Solidarity Worldwide,* 6.6.06

[22] *The Times* (London), 21.11.05

[23] *Asia News* December 2004; *Human Rights Watch,* 1.3.06

[24] *Epoch Times,* 12.11.05

[25] *BBC News*

[26] *ACN UK News,* 11.11.05

[27] *Catholic News Service*

[28] *Asia News,* 30.9.05

[29] *Catholic News Service*

[30] *Asia News,* October 2006

[31] *Asia News,* 2.2.06

[32] *BBC News,* 2.5.06

[33] *World Christian Encyclopedia,* 2001

[34] *ACN News – Königstein* (ACN UK edited version)

[35] *Rapporto 2006*

[36] *Compass Direct News,* 22.5.06

[37] *All India Catholic Union (AICU)*

[38] *Asia News,* August 2005

[39] *Asia News*, September 2005

[40] *Rapporto 2006*

[41] *BBC News*, 7.4.06

[42] *BBC News,* 19.05.06

[43] *BBC News*, 26.3.03

[44] *Compass Direct News*, 12.6.06

[45] *Compass Direct News*

[46] *Compass Direct News*, 12.5.06

[47] *Oasis International Review*, Issue 2

[48] *Compass Direct News*, 22.5.06

[49] *ACN UK News*, 18.1.06

[50] *ACN UK News*, 7.12.04

[51] *ACN UK News*, July–September 2006

[52] *ACN UK News*, 24.10.05

[53] *BBC News*, 10.11.05

[54] *ACN UK News*, 4.1.06

[55] *ACN UK News*, 30.1.06

[56] *ACN UK News*, 31.1.06

[57] *ACN UK News*, 28.3.06

[58] *Zenit News Agency*, March 2006

[59] *ACN UK News*, 19.6.06

[60] *Jerusalem Centre for Public Affairs*

[61] *Rapporto 2006*

[62] *ACN UK Special Report*, May 2005

[63] *Rapporto 2006*

[64] *ACN UK Special Report,* May 2005

[65] *Rapporto 2006*

[66] *Persécutions antichrétiennes dans le monde*, Thomas Grimaux, Aide à l'Eglise en Détresse

[67] *The Daily Telegraph*, September 2005

[68] *Asia News*, December 2005

[69] *Rapporto 2006*

[70] *ACN UK News*, 5.3.06

[71] *Zenit News Agency*, 22.6.06

[72] *Asia News*

[73] *Asia News*

[74] *Rapporto 2006*

[75] *Christian Solidarity Worldwide*

[76] *ACN News UK*, 1.6.06

[77] *L'Osservatore Romano*

[78] *Ansa News*

[79] *Life Site News*
[80] *Asia News*
[81] *Asia News*
[82] *Asia News*
[83] *Asia News*
[84] *ACN Special Report 'Crisis and Faith in Pakistan'*, Spring 2006
[85] *ACN UK News*, 8.3.06 (reporting from Sukkur)
[86] *ACN UK News*, 23.2.06 (reporting from Pakistan)
[87] *Compass Direct News*, 30.6.06
[88] *ACN UK* News, 30.6.06
[89] *Vedomosti*, 14.11.05
[90] *Official website of the Moscow Patriarchate*
[91] *Open Doors International*
[92] *Rapporto 2006*
[93] *Asia News*, 17.5.05
[94] *Compass Direct News*, 4.5.05
[95] *Annals Australasia*, 5.6.06 (*Asia News*)
[96] *ACN UK* Interview
[97] *ACN UK News*, 30.3.06
[98] *Asia News*
[99] *Compass Direct News*
[100] *Asia News*, 21.6.06
[101] *Fides Agency*
[102] *Ansa News*, 14.3.05
[103] *Misna News Agency*
[104] *ACN UK News*, August 2005
[105] *Misna News Agency*, August 2005
[106] *ACN UK News*, 26.9.06
[107] *Ansa News*
[108] *Anatolia News Agency*
[109] *The Economist*, 25.6.06
[110] *ACN UK News*, 11.7.06
[111] *CIA World Fact Book*
[112] *Persécutions antichrétiennes dans le monde*
[113] *Persécutions antichrétiennes dans le monde*
[114] *ACN UK News*, 28.2.06
[115] *Rapporto 2006*
[116] *Rapporto 2006*
[117] *Christian Solidarity Worldwide*, 26.5.06
[118] *ACN UK News*, 4.8.05
[119] *ACN UK News*, 31.12.05

Introducing *Aid to the Church in Need*

Aid to the Church in Need supports the faithful wherever they are persecuted, oppressed or in pastoral need. ACN is a Catholic charity, helping to bring Christ to the world.

ACN was founded on Christmas Day 1947 and is now a universal pastoral charity of the Catholic Church. In 2005 the charity responded to 5,852 requests for aid from bishops and religious superiors in 145 countries.

- Seminarians are trained
- Bibles and religious literature are printed
- Priests and religious are supported
- Refugees are helped
- Churches and chapels are built and restored
- Over 43 million of ACN's *Child's Bible* have been printed in 150 languages
- Religious programmes are broadcast

For regular updates from the suffering Church around the world and to view our full range of books, cards, gifts and music, please log on to your national website.

Thank you for helping to dry the tears of the abandoned Jesus on the crosses of this century
Fr Werenfried van Straaten, O. Praem
founder of *Aid to the Church in Need*

 **Aid to the Church in Need**

Aid to the Church in Need

In the UK

1 Times Square
Sutton
Surrey
SM1 1LF
United Kingdom

Telephone: +44 (0) 20 8642 8668
Email: acn@acnuk.org
Website: www.acnuk.org

In Australia

PO Box 6245
Blacktown DC
NSW 2148
Australia

Telephone: +61 (0) 2 9679 1929
Email: info@aidtochurch.org
Website: www.aidtochurch.org

In Canada

P.O. Box 670, STN H
Montreal
QC H3G 2M6
Canada

Telephone: +1 (1) 800 585 6333
　　　　　or +1 (1) 514 932 0552
Email: info@acn-aed-ca.org
Website: www.acn-aed-ca.org

In Ireland

151 St Mobhi Road
Glasnevin
Dublin 9
Ireland

Telephone: +353 (0) 1 83 77 516
Email: churchinneed@eircom.net
Website: www.acnirl.org

In the USA

725 Leonard Street
PO Box 220384
Brooklyn
NY 11222-0384
USA

Telephone: +1 (1) 800 628 6333
Email: info@acnusa.org
Website: www.churchinneed.com